Remembering South Carolina's

OLD PENDLETON
DISTRICT

Remembering South Carolina's OLD PENDLETON DISTRICT

Best wishes to Frank

[signature]

HURLEY E. BADDERS

Charleston — London

History
PRESS

Published by The History Press
Charleston, SC 29403
www.historypress.net

Front cover: The historic Pendleton Farmers Hall.
Back cover: The 1797 Old Stone Church.
Photos by the author.

First published 2006

Manufactured in the United Kingdom

ISBN-10 1.59629.197.4
ISBN-13 978.1.59629.197.3

Library of Congress Cataloging-in-Publication Data

Badders, Hurley E.
    Remembering South Carolina's old Pendleton District / Hurley E.
Badders.
       p. cm.
  ISBN-13: 978-1-59629-197-3 (alk. paper)
  ISBN-10: 1-59629-197-4 (alk. paper)
 1. Pendleton District (S.C.)--History. 2. Pendleton District
(S.C.)--History--Anecdotes. 3. Pendleton District (S.C.)--History, Local.
4. Anderson County (S.C.)--History. 5. Oconee County (S.C.)--History. 6.
Pickens County (S.C.)--History. I. Title.
  F277.P35B33 2006
  975.7'25--dc22
                            2006027585

For my grandson A.J. Badders and his grandmother, my wife Barbara, the two grandest people in the world!

Contents

Foreword

*W*hen most people think of history their minds turn to major events of the past that occurred somewhere far away. The assassination of Abraham Lincoln, the Great Depression and the Japanese attack on Pearl Harbor are all historic events that impacted millions of people. We frequently forget that history is being made right in our own backyards all the time. Often local history has had as much of an impact on the lives of individuals as the major events of the past. But it is the local history, stories and folklore that are lost because historians do not study them in depth and they are not documented by numerous publications. Rather, their survival is dependent on either the oral tradition or perhaps publication in a little-known work by a local antiquarian.

Remembering South Carolina's Old Pendleton District recounts many of the stories and history of the present-day counties of Anderson, Oconee and Pickens. Readers can learn about the history of Andersonville as a river town or explore ghosts at Hunter's Store in Pendleton or follow the legend of the Indian maiden Issaqueena. There is even a detailed account of three Pendleton brothers and their contributions to the Civil War. Each of these topics relates one small piece of the larger story that is the Old Pendleton District, and no other place in the country can claim the same history. While each area's history is different, there are common threads running through our history that bind us to our state and subsequently to the nation.

It would be difficult to find an individual more qualified to document the history of the Old Pendleton District than Hurley E. Badders. For thirty-six years Hurley, as director of the Pendleton District Historical, Recreational and Tourism Commission, roamed the hills and valleys of the Upcountry region recording the oral traditions as told by lifelong elderly residents across the state. Hurley's research found an outlet in the hundreds of talks he did for students, civic clubs, historical societies and any other group that provided him an opportunity to promote the region's history.

Badders recounts some of the history that should be familiar to Upcountry residents. But he also relates little-known stories of the Old Pendleton District that illustrate why history is so engaging—you can easily visit many of the places where it happened and learn how the incident impacted the evolution of the region.

Rodger D. Stroup, PhD
Director
South Carolina Department of Archives and History

Preface

When I left the newspaper business as a copy boy, then reporter, then news editor, I had never spoken to a group in public. I quickly learned by becoming executive director of the tri-county Pendleton District Historical, Recreational and (later) Tourism Commission that public speaking was part of the job.

The first invitation came less than a month after I was on the job, and it for was a ladies' group in Easley. I was a nervous wreck and, to make matters worse, one of the members was a woman I knew and greatly liked. She only corrected me three times while I was on the floor talking (and almost literally on the floor, passing out in fright).

A few weeks later, I had basically memorized one talk (I don't do speeches) and had been invited to speak with the Seneca Rotary Club. A Clemson University dean who lived in Pendleton was making up a missed meeting and afterward he came up, welcomed me to Pendleton and had a nice chat with me. Rotary Clubs must have a network because two weeks later I was invited to the Clemson club where this particular dean was a member. I told him he was going to hear the same thing, and he said that was good, as he had missed a few points in my first talk. Two weeks later I was at the Anderson club, and he appeared at the door. I nodded my head, he shook his and turned and left.

Preface

When I retired thirty-six years later, I had learned other subjects and did not need notes as I spoke. It seems when you live in the past daily, that past becomes ingrained in your mind, making it easy to spout out times and places. So here are some of those talks, ones people asked if I would put in book form. Enjoy!

In the Beginning

The world was dark and wet and flat and the animals put fire on a track and raised it so it would come up on one side and hours later would descend on the other side. The buzzard flew for miles to find a good place to live, and as its wings would hit the muddy surface, it created a valley and the upraised wings caused mountains to form. It became the land of the Cherokee Indians.

Folklore of the Cherokees, as well as other races in all nations, has always been an important part of our past. While some of the tales certainly don't resemble the truth, the stories have survived the times. These tales and a few names of Cherokee origin are all that is left in the northwestern corner of South Carolina to remind us of the great nation that once called the region home.

Animals were always the key figures in the Cherokee tales. Fire, for example, came when the thunder sent the lightning, which struck a tree, setting it aflame. The raven went to bring back some of the fire, got too close and its wings were scorched—and they look that way today. The hoot owl tried and was hit by a blast of light from the fire. The hoot owl would not open its eyes in light thereafter. Finally, the spider spun a web to make a bowl, put the hot coals on its back and brought it home, and we have had fire ever since. The spider has also had a red spot on its back ever since.

Table Rock Mountain in Pickens County got its name from an Indian legend that said a giant Cherokee ate from the mountaintop while sitting on a smaller mountain. It is at Table Rock State Park on South Carolina Highway 11. *Photo by the author.*

The great Cherokee Indian nation was well organized. It consisted of three divisions, similar to our states. The capital was near present-day Cherokee, North Carolina, in what was known as the Overhill towns. The vicinity of what is now Franklin, North Carolina, was in the Middle Towns, and the Lower Towns composed present-day Anderson, Greenville, Oconee and Pickens Counties. In pre-British times the Cherokee land went as far as present-day Columbia.

The capital of the Lower Towns was the Place of the Mulberries, known by its Cherokee name as Keowee. It was a thriving town when Hernando De Soto and his Spanish explorers visited there in 1539, and it was still the capital when the British built Fort Prince George across the river in 1753.

Most of the major towns in the Lower Towns were on the rivers in present-day Oconee and Pickens Counties, although smaller towns were located throughout the region, but often only for short periods. They lived in places like the Sunlight of the Gods (Tamassee in the Cherokee language), Green Parrot (Eastatoe) and Place Where the Duck Fell Off (Coneross). They fished on rivers such as the Two (Tugaloo), the High Uplifted Waters (Chauga) and the Rocky Waters (Chattooga). Many of their towns were in the Water Eyes of the Hills, derived from the Cherokee word Uk-oo-na, now spelled Cherokee.

Names were always descriptive. Tamassee was a magical chief who wore a giant sparkling red ruby around his neck. Ducks would rest on a ledge over a creek and when they flew away, wind currents would cause them to descend a few feet—therefore, it was where the duck fell off. The numerous streams in the mountains certainly could be water eyes.

Maize, or corn, was the primary crop of the Cherokees. The fish they caught often were used as fertilizer for the corn. They hunted deer, buffalo (numerous here at one time), turkeys, bears, wild boars and small game. The Cherokees, despite the Hollywood image and the tourist attractions in North Carolina, did not live in tepees. They lived in log houses. A single feather in the hair, not a ground-length bonnet, distinguished the chief. Roots, tree bark and leaves made up most of the remedies for ailments, covering everything from headaches to abortions. Corn was ground into mush and was oftentimes fried or eaten as stew.

Soon after the colony of Carolina was established by Great Britain in 1670, trade relations began with the Cherokees and tribes like the Congarees and Catawabas in other parts of what now is South Carolina. Furs were carried to Charles Towne and made quite a hit—and a lot of money for the British—when shipped to England. Traders began coming into the region and the Cherokees were getting along fine with the white man—for a while.

In 1753 Royal Governor James Glen came to the Eastatoe area, met with the Cherokee chiefs and showed friendship by saying the Royal government would build a fort across the river from Keowee to protect the Cherokees from the warring Creek Indians in what is now Georgia. Glen didn't say this, but it also was to protect the British from the Cherokees.

Trade relations were getting thin. The Cherokees felt they were being cheated and several deaths occurred, prompting the Indians to declare war against the British in 1759. Royal troops sailed from New York to Charles Town and then marched into Cherokee country. The war of 1759–60 resulted in the Cherokees being on the losing end, so they pledged their allegiance to "our father, the King of England."

The Broken Path Is Fixed

Histories of the American Revolution in South Carolina rarely, if ever, mention a key event in the war that opened the last frontier of the state. In 1976 I published a small book called *Broken Path: The Cherokee Campaign of 1776*. It was also one of my talks to groups. Long out of print, it bears summarizing here.

The allegiance given by the Cherokees to the king after the war of 1759–60 proved to be the downfall of the Lower Towns. With the American Revolution brewing, the Cherokees agreed to side with the Loyalists and the British in fighting the revolutionaries. That engagement came to be because a British commissioner had urged the Cherokees on, telling them they ought not to turn against their father, the king, but should join with the attacks, which began on settlements on July 1, 1776. It fell to the task of Major Andrew Williamson to muster the militia for retaliation. A contemporary magazine article said the militia galloped away to attack immediately. Not so.

Forces began to gather at Ninety Six in what now is Greenwood County on July 2, and two days later 40 were ready to march. By July 5, there were 110 assembled and the hardy band inched forward as they reached DeWitt's Corner at the very edge of the Indian nation.

(Let's digress here for a moment. DeWitt's Corner was a trading post and is so shown on early maps. A few years later a new map

Oconee Station, north of Walhalla off South Carolina Scenic Highway 11, was likely built prior to 1760 as an outpost. It is part of the South Carolina Department of Parks, Recreation and Tourism. *Photo by the author.*

was published and the word "corner" apparently wouldn't fit, so it was listed as "DeWitt's." Still later, a mapmaker possibly couldn't read too well and the new map showed it as "Duetts." Finally, more modern maps came along; the name had become "Due West." That's where Erskine College is located and it isn't due west of anything in particular.)

Now back to our story.

On July 26, coming over a ridge from Six and Twenty Mile Creek the Rebels set up an early base camp—1,154 of them now. It had taken nearly a month to travel almost sixty miles—hardly a gallop—and they were in the vicinity of where Interstate 85 now crosses U.S. 76 north of Anderson.

The striking hour came on the night of July 31 when Williamson picked three hundred horsemen and crossed the valley of Eighteen Mile Creek to attack the Seneca Village (not the present town of

Seneca). The major himself led the group, with Captain Andrew Pickens of the Long Canes and his men immediately in the rear. Williamson's men were at a fence surrounding the village in the dark of the night, and as they lowered the fence bars Indians and Tories dressed as Indians opened fire. The opening shots were to strike down the first person of the Jewish faith to die for America.

Francis Salvador, born to affluent parents in London in 1757, may have never come to these shores but for the family overspeculating in the East India spice trade. Undaunted by the financial loss, Salvador turned his attention to six thousand acres of land, which had been acquired in the Ninety Six area by family members some years earlier. In 1773 young Francis saw a profitable future in crop growing and his place came to be called Cornacre. The community of Coronace (see, the spelling changed!) shows on maps today.

The people of Ninety Six had elected Salvador to the First and Second Provisional Congresses in 1775–76. While the British were attacking Charles Town, Salvador was helping Williamson round up the militia. Andrew Pickens, a cousin of the more famous captain and later general of the same name, left a graphic account of what happened when the Seneca Village was attacked.

He wrote that when the ambush began, ten or twelve militiamen fell wounded, Salvador among them. He was described as a young man of great attractiveness and was "beautifully dressed in a white uniform." Williamson himself was plainly dressed, and the chronicler Pickens said the Loyalists and Cherokees must have thought Salvador was the commander. The white uniform was reddening now, Salvador having been wounded three times. An Indian approached to scalp him and Pickens wrote that another militiaman thought it was Salvador's servant coming to aid him. Salvador lived forty-five minutes, never losing consciousness.

Williamson's horse had been wounded and he managed to get Salvador's horse and continue the battle. Pickens and his men had moved forward and some order was achieved. The Indians took to the trees and firing continued until the enemy retreated for good. Three of Williamson's men had died, including Salvador, and they were buried there. Others were wounded and died en route home and many of the wounded would never see battle again. Salvador's family had his remains removed to London, and there are statues and plaques commemorating him in London, Washington and Charleston.

Daylight came shortly after the battle and the militia could see the village well. Naturalist William Bartram had been there a year earlier and wrote in his diary, "The Cherokee town of Sinica is a very respectful settlement, situated on the east bank of the Keowee River, though the greatest number of Indian inhabitations are on the opposite shore, where likewise stands the councilhouse in a level twixt the river and a range of beautifully lofty hills…but the chief's house, with those of the traders, and some Indian dwellings, are situated on the ascent of the opposite shore."

Williamson's force saw much of the same but with no habitation. The militia burned the entire town, and the crops of corn were destroyed after the men had provisioned themselves. With nothing left standing, the troops turned back to their camps on Six and Twenty Creek and Eighteen Mile Creek and began attacks on other Cherokee towns. Williamson with 640 men marched on Oconee and, finding no one there, moved on to Osttatoy and Tugaloo, destroying both as they went. On August 11, Indian towns and provisions were destroyed on Brasstown stream. Spartan region (now Spartanburg) forces had gathered in the meantime, mainly striking at the Cherokees and British sympathizers in the vicinity of present-day Greenville.

Moving on, the Spartans joined Williamson at Keowee, across from the former Fort Prince George. Indian towns were destroyed as they went. Williamson's force reached Tomassee—not to be confused with Tamassee—on August 12 where Captain Andrew Pickens and his lifelong friend Robert Anderson were searching for the enemy. Hand-to-hand combat resulted when they found the enemy, and after Williamson's men and the main body arrived, some order was restored and sixteen dead Indians were found in a 150-yard space.

Chehoee and Eustash were added to the list of towns destroyed, and all crops were wiped out. Back to the main camp the troops went, and some were allowed furloughs until August 26, when they were to meet with those remaining at Seneca Town. (There's something about Indian village names. Seneca, for example, was also listed on maps as Sinica, Senica, Sinika and Essenneca. Maybe it was the mapmakers who did it?)

On their return they found that Williamson and the 600 men who remained with him had constructed a small post near the ruins of the town. It had been named Fort Rutledge in honor of state President John Rutledge. (The DAR placed a small stone replica of the fort at the site, now rarely seen in the growth and access to the unmarked site.) By September 11, and with a force that had grown to 2,300 at Fort Rutledge and on Eighteen Mile Creek, Williamson—now a colonel—moved into the Cherokee Middle settlement in the Franklin, North Carolina area to aid General Rutherford of North Carolina for additional Indian attacks.

As October approached the Cherokees were defeated and with frost in the air, Williamson and his men returned to their homes. Ninety-nine militiamen had died, more than two thousand Indians breathed no more and a questionable peace was at hand. The Cherokees had been listening to Andrew Cameron, the British commissioner who had urged them into battle, but he was not to be found. At the height of the Williamson campaign he had escaped to Florida.

On February 3, 1777, in Charleston, hearings were held regarding the Cherokees, and the tribe had sent one official representative and another who wanted to be heard. Byrd was the official spokesman and he told the Privy Council: "The Great Man above has put all of us down on the earth, and He did not know why we quarreled and he sent down fire and spoiled the path, but hoped it would be clear again." Mankiller, on the other hand, did not go to Charleston as a messenger but on his own accord. He said he had met with Williamson, who he called Warrior Beloved Man, and had good talks with him. He said that formerly his Great Father, meaning the King of England, had made the path strong but now it was broken. He said his brothers had destroyed the homes of the Indians but it was not their fault—it was the fault of the Great Father who lived over the Great Water. He wanted the broken path repaired. The Privy Council was impressed and set up a treaty to be acted on at DeWitt's Corner. The treaty was established on March 20, 1777, and the Cherokees yielded their claim to what became the Pendleton District and now are Anderson, Oconee and Pickens Counties. The broken path was fixed.

What of Andrew Williamson? He rose to the rank of general and campaigned in Georgia and at Stono where his actions were slow and evasive. Arrested, he was charged with treason and it was believed that he had taken a commission in the British army. In McCall's history of Georgia, Williamson is accused of tipping off Alexander Cameron of the attack at Seneca Town. History has never decided, but Williamson is recorded by many as the Benedict Arnold of the South.

And what of the proud Cherokees, who had fought so valiantly for their king, but fell in defeat, then took up arms for America? Robert Mills, the famed architect who designed the Washington Monument and so many important buildings, in his *Statistics of South Carolina* in 1828 described the Pendleton District thus: "A few years only have elapsed since these mountains and valleys were the property and abode of the Indians…the Indians have retired to the other side of the mountains. They occasionally visit the district in little bands, to dig up pink root, which grows in great abundance in these mountains. They carry with them a small hoe fit for the purpose, encamp in the woods under mean hovels made of bark, subsisting upon the casual produce of the chase, and the pittance they beg amongst the settlers."

How the Opossum Got Its Tail

The small American marsupial, which lives in trees but mostly is seen along the roadside (usually flat), is generally known in the Southland as a plain old possum, not even the correct name opossum. The Cherokees knew how it gets its tail, and therein lies a tale.

In the days of the animals, they all lived happily together. The possum had the biggest, bushiest tail of any animal, and—as the story goes—it was quick to brag about it constantly. The animals grew weary of hearing the tail tale almost every day. The boasting days would soon be over, however.

The animals had planned a dance, and all of them wanted to look their best. The cricket was the barber of the animals—remember, this is a legend—and several of the animals conspired to play a trick on the possum. Sure enough, the possum came rushing up to the cricket, asking that his big, beautiful, bushy tail be done up right for the dance. The cricket said he would do a special trim and would wrap it in ribbon, which the possum could not unravel until the dance. Without the possum knowing it, the cricket shaved off all the hair on the tail, and then hid it with the ribbon.

That night, it was time for the dance. The possum came bouncing out, singing with glee about his beautiful tail. He then unwrapped the ribbon in front of all the animals, and they broke into laughter. The possum turned back and looked, saw a long, hairless red tail and turned on his side and started grinning…and he's been grinning ever since.

Skyagunsta

$\mathscr{L}$ ike most of the state, the upper part of South Carolina is blessed with the number of people from other parts of the nation—and the world—who have moved in and become an important part of their new community. Actually, it's a case of history repeating itself.

Certainly the first settlers had to come from somewhere else, and later generations born here can trace their family back to some other state or nation. Just as many "newcomers" were making their mark in the region, there were some who stood tall at the beginning, too.

Let's consider a native in the Paxton Township of Pennsylvania. His parents arrived there from Ireland, later moved to Virginia and finally to the Waxhaws, near present-day Lancaster, South Carolina. By the time he grew to manhood, a farmer with a wife and small children, he moved into the Long Canes, now Abbeville, South Carolina, and after making a name for himself during the American Revolution, he moved into what would become the Pendleton District.

His name was Andrew Pickens.

As a young man, Pickens fought with the British during the Cherokee War in 1759–60, and he was a captain in the state militia in 1776 when he went back into Indian territory, fighting the Cherokees

Andrew Pickens's home dates to the 1780s and is near Clemson and Pendleton. It was the site of treaties with several Indian nations in 1785 and 1786. *Photo by the author.*

and pro-British. When the British took South Carolina later in the war, he went back to farming and tried to sit out the conflict.

A devout man, Pickens felt he should honor the oath he was required to take—the oath of allegiance to the British not to fight—but when raiding parties all but destroyed his farm in the Long Canes, he was ready to fight again. As a colonel, he rounded up supporters and headed for the Cowpens, where General Daniel Morgan and his Patriot forces were facing a superior foe, led by the dreaded Green Dragoon Banastre Tarleton.

Pickens's maneuvering at the Cowpens resulted in a rout of the British, pushing them back into North Carolina—and coupled with success at Kings Mountain—all the way to Yorktown, where the British surrendered. Pickens's actions resulted in a gift of a commemorative sword from the Continental Congress and a promotion to brigadier general. Other military actions followed, and with Francis "Swamp Fox" Marion and Thomas "Gamecock" Sumter, Pickens was hailed as one of the great partisan generals of the South. All three are in the South Carolina Hall of Fame.

Pickens mostly was a peaceful man, however, and he liked frontier life. As settlers began moving into the Long Canes after the war, he found it getting crowded and acquired property in 1785 on the Keowee River—later called the Seneca River and now known as Lake Hartwell. He built a home, still standing although modernized. It is on the eastern shore of the lake near Clemson.

Before the home could be completed, the new American government called on Pickens to draw up treaties with the Southern Indian tribes during the winter of 1785–86 on his property. There were Cherokee, Choctaw and Chickasaw nations in attendance. Pickens remained as an Indian commissioner for twenty years, helping establish the boundaries of most of the Southern states. So impressed with his coolness and fairness, the Indians gave him the name Skyagunsta, meaning Border Wizard Owl.

The general stayed busy in other matters, too. He was a commissioner to establish Pendleton County (later District) and was on the commission that selected Columbia for the state capital. He

Old Stone Church, burial place of many founders of the Pendleton area, is on U.S. Highway 76 between Clemson and Pendleton. *Photo by the author.*

served in Congress (often walking to Washington and back), and he started Hopewell-on-the-Keowee Presbyterian Church, which burned; it was rebuilt in 1797 as the Stone Meeting House and is today's Old Stone Church.

William Martin, a neighbor, once described Pickens: "He was in height about 5 ft, 10 inches—quite lean and slender—quite ugly—with strong and commanding features...grave, seldom smiled, never laughed, pious, conversed but little, and by no means freely...except with particular friends, and of them, he was remarkably choice...A gentleman once referring to him said that when he was about to speak, he would first take the words out of his mouth, between his fingers, and examine them before uttering them."

A son, Ezekial, was lieutenant governor of South Carolina (1802– 04); another son, Andrew, was governor (1816–18); and a grandson,

Francis W., was governor (1860–62) when South Carolina seceded from the Union.

When Pendleton became crowded, General Pickens moved to his Red House at Tamassee, near where he had battled the Cherokees in 1776. He died there December 19, 1814, sitting under a tree and reading his mail. His beloved wife Becky had died earlier and was buried at the Stone Meeting House, and he was returned there beside her.

The Deer's Head

There have been numerous versions of a popular tale about the Indian maiden Issaqueena, which means Deer's Head in the Creek language or Cateechee in the Cherokee language.

As the story goes, which is a better way of saying "once upon a time," there was a beautiful young maiden (they always are) who lived with her family in Keowee Town in what now is Oconee County. Traders from Star Fort visited her area often and one, whose last name was Francis (several different first names have been used over the years), had caught her eye and she fell in love with him. One night, she overheard the chief and braves plotting a plan to attack Star Fort and, fearing for Mr. Francis's life, she jumped on her horse. Using the counting beads around her neck and checking her mileage every time she crossed a stream, she galloped off to Star Fort to warn him. From her home at Keowee, she went one mile, where One Mile Creek in Pickens County is located today, then on to Twelve Mile River, Eighteen Mile Creek, Three and Twenty Mile Creek, Six and Twenty Mile Creek and finally arrived at Star Fort, ninety-six miles away.

Let's interrupt this tale for a moment to analyze this much: those creeks exist today in Pickens and Anderson Counties, the national historical site Star Fort is located in the Greenwood County town of Ninety Six and they are generally the same distance apart from the now-underwater Keowee town. There was one other stream along the way named Hen Coop, located in Abbeville County. A well-respected Anderson historian, who was also an accountant, researched the name for many years and finally determined it was a Cherokee Indian name pronounced "hon-coo," meaning "how far?" (remember—this is a true or false story).

Now back to the story.

Issaqueena saved the day for the Star Fort people, married Mr. Francis and they moved back into the mountains a few miles from Keowee into a giant hollowed-out tree, which the Indians called a "stump house." After the proper time span, she became a mother and was out picking berries with other Indian females and her baby on her back. Lonesome for her traveling husband and still not trusted by the Cherokees, she took advantage of a sudden heavy rainfall, ran to the top of the waterfalls and jumped. One version of the ending, an extremely long and boring poem, tells of how the mother and child fell to their deaths.

The more popular version, however, is one that has a happy ending: Issaqueena jumped to a ledge some ten feet from the top, hid behind the falls until dark and then made her way through the forest to finally be reunited with her spouse. Some have advanced a theory that they moved to Alabama, where he traded with Indians and became an Alabama legislator when the United States came into being. That does make a better ending than the gruesome one.

Some final observations: Old maps do show a stump house near the falls, which came to be known as Issaqueena Falls. By the way, it's on Stump House Mountain, so how did the mountain get its name?

Party-poopers say a newspaperman fabricated the story in the early twentieth century, and the naysayers say they bet the traders who frequented the area named the streams.

Some of you readers will say that's not the way you heard it and have variations to tell. Go ahead, that's the glory of storytelling.

Finally: true or false? You decide.

Printer John Miller

An Englishman who came to Pendleton before there was a Pendleton played an important part in establishing freedom of the press in the United States. He also played a role in the creation and development of the Pendleton District and brought with him from England a cure for snakebite.

Printer John Miller, toward the close of a busy career, was publishing one of the westernmost newspapers in the nation when he began circulating his *Miller's Weekly Messenger* in 1807 in Pendleton. He was better received here than in London, where he spent a lot of time in jail for his publishing efforts.

A publisher of several London newspapers during his years there, Miller was one of several journalists who printed the "Letters of Junius," anonymously written attacks on the Royal government and sometimes the King of England himself; it landed him in jail each time.

Miller and several other journalists found refuge in the new United States, and when he arrived in Philadelphia in January 1783, South Carolina's delegates to Congress befriended him and invited him to start a newspaper in Charleston. The stories he, as well as other newspapermen told, likely led to freedom of the press being written into our Bill of Rights.

In the second issue of his *South Carolina Gazette and General Advertiser* on March 22, 1783, Miller explained how he was "placed so soon and so remotely as in the State of South Carolina." His views had turned to agriculture, "which so far as public service would permit" had been a "favorite employment" for several years. "The news of the evacuation of Charles-town had just been received when I reached Philadelphia," Miller wrote, "and your Hon. Delegates in Congress did me the honour to conceive me to Charles-town to become your printer." He went on to explain just what his beliefs were by quoting what he told Lord Mansfield in 1783 "on receiving sentence previous to my last imprisonment" in London.

Miller's statement was, "My Lord, I have served the public fifteen years faithfully and disinterestedly, eight years of which I laboured in defending and asserting the rights of my countrymen and fellow citizens!—and the last seven years in decrying and exposing the WICKEDNESS and the FOLLY of the ACCURSED AMERICAN WAR!!" The colonists in this new nation loved him for that statement and others like it.

Printer Miller had been seeking to have South Carolina's Henry Laurens released from a London prison, the American diplomat having been charged with treason by the British, but Miller wound up there before Laurens was out. This time, however, did not concern a Junius letter. He had "inadvertently" copied from another newspaper a paragraph reflecting on the character of the Russian ambassador to England. Miller tried to apologize, saying it was highly improbable that "the Empress of all the Russias would go to war with the King of Britain because John Miller told a lie about her ambassador."

The court didn't agree, and he went off to jail for a one-year term, cut to less than half that time after a short-lived Whig government took control over the Tory government and released him. That did it; Miller decided to leave his native land. He tried Ireland for a few months, saw he would be no better there and struck out for America with his wife and seven children.

In Charleston, everything was not necessarily rosy. His newspaper there altered in name a couple of times and frequency of publication altered with it. Miller had been classed as a radical in England, but in America he showed conservative tendencies, often refusing to print radical contributions. For this and his foreign birth, he was frequently denounced.

The legislature in 1785 was swayed to giving preference to an American press, and foreigner Miller sold the newspaper. Once again he wanted to turn his attention to agriculture. He acquired 640 acres of land on Eighteen Mile Creek between present-day Pendleton and Clemson, when it was a part of the Ninety Six District before Pendleton came into being. There were but a few settlers in the region at the time, but it soon would change.

Agriculture and politics took up Miller's time for several years. He was appointed a commissioner to found Pendleton County, helping to select the site for a courthouse, and he was elected the first clerk of court. Miller was an organizer and quite a vocal member of the Pendleton Franklin Society, an anti-Federalist group concerned with the new nation's policies. He wrote and spoke often on political matters, and one particular comment was "laziness in politics is like laziness in agriculture; it exposes the soil to noxious weeds."

A neighbor and fellow Pendleton commissioner was the Patriot General Andrew Pickens. When Pickens and other early settlers desired to build a lasting Presbyterian church (the first one had burned), Miller gave the land for the Stone Meeting House, started in 1797 and completed in 1802. A lasting edifice it was; it stands today between Pendleton and Clemson and is more commonly known as the Old Stone Church.

Printer's ink can often replace blood in newspapermen. It could have been that blood—or possibly a wait until there were a sufficient number of people living in Pendleton to be subscribers—but in 1807 printer John Miller went back into the newspaper business. *Miller's Weekly Messenger* was started in January 1807. It was the westernmost newspaper in the United States at the time. It was in the fine service of a growing population who had no other way to learn the news of the world. Miller, except for his local accounts, followed the common practice of the day by reprinting articles from larger newspapers, which arrived by stage weeks after the occurrence.

An often-told story of the day is that one week some of the town's youngsters slipped into the print shop and changed one letter in the title—with the issue coming out as "Miller's Weakly Messenger." The name was later changed to the *Pendleton Messenger*.

Printer John Miller died on Thursday, November 26, 1807. His son, John, wrote the obituary and promised to carry on the newspaper, which he did, with his son John following him until the newspaper was sold in 1820. Printer John is buried in the Old Stone Church cemetery, his resting place barely distinguishing a unique individual who played a leader's role in the early development of the region.

An article in the July 4, 1789 issue of the *Philadelphia Monthly Magazine* was written by printer John Miller, and with it he left something for future generations to consider. He wrote to tell of a cure for snakebite, one he remembered from his days in London when viper-catchers for chemists and apothecaries were often bitten. He wrote that in 1786, shortly after coming to Pendleton, a rattlesnake bit a man. Miller forced the cure down the victim's throat, coated the man's legs and feet with the remedy and said in two hours' time the man's swelling subsided. Miller said he used the cure often after that, and the results were always gratifying. The cure? It came from a bottle but it was not the kind of liquid often identified with rattlesnake bites.

Printer John Miller used a bottle of castor oil.

How Many Pendletons?

*J*ust which Pendleton are you looking for? There's the Town of Pendleton, Pendleton County, Pendleton District, Pendleton Historic District and more, including the Pendleton Woolen Mills, but that's another story to be addressed further along.

The Town of Pendleton was created in 1789, the same year Pendleton County was formed out of a briefly lived Washington District. The Pendleton District came along in 1800, gaining judicial status when the state legislature changed its mind in one of several times to come. A small courthouse and jail had been built for the county, and with judicial status a larger courthouse and jail was erected on the brand new village green. (Don't you wonder why a jail is always one of the first things a new entity erects?)

Most people would say it's a town square in the middle of town, but the beauty of the area and the historic significance deserve the village green status. To mix things up further, the Pendleton Historic District was designated on the National Register of Historic Places in 1971 and national—even international—attention came to the area, which included the town itself and a small area east and west of town. You'll find it listed in major travel guides.

But what about the Pendleton District? Not to be confused with the other Pendletons, it was basically the last frontier of South Carolina, the northwest corner that had belonged to the Cherokee Indians. The legislature, likely having fun as it changed the rules again, split the Pendleton District in half in 1828, creating Anderson District and Pickens District, named for the Revolutionary War luminaries. There'll be more on that later, as well as a few details on the Pendleton District Historical, Recreational and Tourism Commission.

Confused? A written test may be given.

Let's not forget the Washington District. It was created out of the former Cherokee Indian nation and its courthouse was first named Rockville, and then changed to Pickensville to honor the general. It was located adjacent to the present Easley Fire Department and naturally a jail was also built. It was an underground jail carved from the rock, which was considerable in that area. It appears to have been swallowed up by progress, in this case called Wal-Mart.

The former Indian territory was made a part of the just created Ninety Six District, and then became Abbeville County. In 1789 the legislature took the Indian land and created a district named for George Washington. Two counties were carved out a year later, Greenville and Pendleton. The former was named for General Nathaniel Greene, commander of the Southern Patriot forces in the Revolution, and the last was named for Judge Henry Pendleton, a Virginia native who fought alongside Greene and stayed in the state after the war. Pendleton, who made his new home in what now is lower Greenville County, championed the causes for the "back country." Charleston ran the state in those days and didn't even want to acknowledge that people lived elsewhere.

But back to the Town of Pendleton. Lowcountry planters and politicians discovered the town, as it was free of the bugs and heat of their normal homes. Some of the most influential citizens of the times moved there for the summer and some stayed. R.W. Simpson wrote in the early 1900s that in the "early 1800s the very name of Pendleton became a synonym for refined and beautiful women and for elegant high-toned and chivalrous gentlemen."

The commissioners of the new Pendleton County met for the first time on April 8, 1790, to purchase land on which to erect the county buildings and to select John Miller as the clerk of court. The next day the commissioners met again to plan roads in the county, as none existed except for the old Cherokee Path to Charleston. The commissioners, by the way, were Andrew Pickens, Robert Anderson, John Miller, John Wilson, Benjamin Cleveland, William Halbert, Henry Clark and John Moffett. They determined each road should lead from Pendleton to or by their homes. (Imagine politicians getting away with that now!) It worked well, however, as they lived in all parts of the county. (Observation: Tri-County Technical College is located in Pendleton and all but one of the original buildings is named for the commissioners. The auditorium building, however, is named Oconee because people there said Anderson and Pickens were named, so their county should be recognized. Peace must be kept, particularly when all three counties furnish the funding for the college.)

In 1800 the legislature determined there should be a new system of courts, and the Pendleton District came into being. The commissioners then started formally laying out lots. It resulted in fifty-one town lots of one acre each and forty-three lots of varying acreage. Some lots had been sold earlier and the numbers were added later. One of the first to come, in 1790, was William Steele, who opened a store and also became postmaster. The building stands today and is a restaurant. (Imagine a map of the United States and where Pendleton is located. The post office was the westernmost in the United States at the time). Pickensville no longer existed and the only named places were Pendleton, Pumpkintown and Andersonville. Pumpkintown remains as a small community almost at the foot of the mountains and Andersonville, now an island, is treated elsewhere.

One of the most magnificent dwellings in the town is Lowther Hall, which sits on the highest spot in town. When it was still Pendleton County, the hall was built by Dr. William Hunter, obviously a pioneer because the area was so new. The Hunters lived there until 1805. About that time a lawyer named William Shaw appeared and said he was representing a Lord Lowther. He actually was—more correctly—the Right Honorable William Lord Viscount Lowther, one of the Lords of the Treasury of Great Britain, a commissioner for the affairs of India, etc., etc., etc. Foreigners could not own land at that time in America (boy, has that changed!) and Shaw was to be his agent, but all interests were then deeded to William Broadfoot of Charleston to hold for the use of Lord Lowther.

The property consisted of "the capitol mansion house and buildings consisting of two housekeeper or scullery rooms, kitchen scullery, smoke or dairy house, poultry house, pidgeon house, carriage house and stable." All that was on five hundred acres of land. The tradition with the old-timers, and maybe some younger ones, is that Lord Lowther built a hunting lodge in Pendleton and on a return to England to get his bride, he died at sea.

Nope. What has been said above is straight from the official records. It is doubtful Lord Lowther ever saw the property as Shaw was doing the same thing in other counties, representing British royalty, and in later years the property became involved in legal snarls and changed hands a number of times, once becoming the Masonic Temple. Privately owned and without most of the early acreage, the house is lovingly maintained by its owner.

The town has two house museums. Lewis Ladson Gibbes built one, Ashtabula, in 1828, or so the cornerstone says. Actually, he died that year and his wife had died in 1826. She was a member of the Drayton and Middleton families. They had eight children, who sold the property in 1837 to Dr. Ozey Robert Broyles, whose interest in agriculture led him to invent a subsoil plow, and he also wrote papers for farm magazines. In 1851 the place was purchased by James T. Latta, whose son Edward Dilworth Latta became a well-known industrialist in Charlotte and Asheville, North Carolina. In 1862 Robert Adger bought the property for his daughter, Clarissa (later Mrs. O.W. Bowen, who kept a detailed diary about Pendleton during the Civil War). Textile executive Francis J. Pelzer acquired the property and began a Jersey stock farm known throughout the South. Other owners followed and the house has never been vacant since it was built.

Across town is the massive Woodburn Plantation house museum. It was built circa 1830 by Charles Cotesworth Pinckney, the lieutenant governor of South Carolina in 1833. He wasn't the only Charles Cotesworth Pinckney, as several generations of the notable Charleston family carried that name. His brother, Thomas, who had been governor of the state, was already in Pendleton at his home, Altamont. C.C. bought several tracts of land adjoining each other on Eighteen Mile Creek. He built a four-story house with several outbuildings and he remained there until 1852. He then sold all his Pendleton property and returned to Charleston, where he died in 1865.

John Bailey Adger then purchased the property in Pendleton and gave it its name, from a couplet of a Walter Scott poem: "Where Reed upon her margin sees / Sweet Woodburn's cottage and trees." He and his wife had spent twelve years in Asia as missionaries where his main work was to translate the Bible into the modern language of the Armenians. Then, recovering from a long illness and with failing eyesight, he became a missionary for five years to the black people of Charleston. In Pendleton on Sundays while he went about the countryside preaching, his wife would gather the children and adults of the slaves and read the Bible and teach hymns to them. Regaining his health, Adger sold Woodburn in 1858, spent seventeen years at the Columbia Theological Seminary and each summer he preached in Pendleton, where he had bought the Boscobel Plantation (now a golf course). Family members and others from the Charleston area were refugees there and at other Pendleton plantations during the Civil War. In Adger's retirement, he returned to Pendleton in 1873 where he wrote: "I enjoyed a long and fruitful pastorate as the resident minister of Pendleton Church."

After several changes in ownership, Woodburn was sold in 1881 to Augustus T. Smythe, an Adger relative, who started a model racehorse farm. Later owners came along and, although the property was mainly remembered as the residence of influential Lowcountry people, the daughter of a former slave and a mother who was born the day President Lincoln signed the Emancipation Proclamation is the only person with a historical marker at the site. She was Jane Edna Hunter, whose death in 1971 brought headlines across America. She left Pendleton as a young woman and settled in

Cleveland, Ohio, where she struggled to find work. When she finally did after getting a nurse's degree, she knew firsthand how difficult it was for young black girls facing a similar future. She started the Phillis Wheatley Association for young black girls, teaching them service skills, cooking, sewing, housekeeping and the like and providing them protected, clean housing at virtually whatever they could pay when employed. All this and her upbringing were recited in her autobiography, *Nickel and a Prayer*.

Many years later under other ownerships, the property came into the hands of the federal government, which turned it over to Clemson College. Clemson deeded it to the Pendleton Historic Foundation in 1966 and restoration began. Today it is a popular place for tours, weddings and other special events. The foundation owns and operates both house museums. An interesting point is that both houses have the so-called widow's walk, normally seen at the seashore and used there for family members to watch ships come in. In this case, it was for the residents to view the Blue Ridge Mountains in the distance, and for a while the Woodburn residents could see the progress on building Clemson College a short distance away.

Adjacent to Woodburn is the Pendleton District Agricultural Museum, which features pre-1925 farm artifacts. Anderson County Senator T. Ed Garrison obtained $65,000 to have the museum built. It resembles a two-story racehorse barn that had been on Woodburn property, but is actually a metal building with vinyl siding. There were no funds for setting up the museum so the interior painting, display panels, lettering and other labor required was done by me, my wife and my daughter with occasional help from D.R. Chastain of Williamston. On opening day we rented one of those disgusting portable signs and put it on the highway where everyone heading to the Clemson football game that day could not help but notice it. The number of people who came in: zero. The sign was still there the next week and attendance improved; two people came in. The museum has been popular with school groups and senior citizens, the latter remembering using this tool or handling that plow. One man, seeing a scythe mounted on the wall, used a few four-letter words and said, "I didn't ever want to see one of those again."

When the town was being developed and a courthouse and jail were erected on the village green, problems erupted over the jail. It was located at the edge of the green and when ladies walked by the prisoners would poke their heads though the bars and say rude and unkind things to them. The grand jury finally took note of this and had the jail moved to a new location off the green. Robert Mills, the man who designed the Washington monument and many other government buildings along with churches, was the state engineer and he had charge of the design and construction. It was two stories with eighteen-inch-thick walls and steel plating. It only served a few years as the Pendleton District was being split in half into Anderson and Pickens Districts, and of course each had to have its own jail as a top priority. There was an immediate need for the empty jail, however, as it was purchased and became the Pendleton Female Academy. (I could make a funny about that, but the ladies wouldn't think it was funny, would they?)

Every town has its special people and Pendleton certainly had its share. One man in the early 1900s would take his cow to the village green every day and let it graze there. Another story involves the lady I'm mentioning now, and even though she chastised me in front of a church sanctuary full of tourists, she was teaching me something. I had been taking a group on tour and this dear lady of the older type was in the first row, apparently checking on me. I mentioned the cemetery and she jumped to her feet, shook her cane and announced loudly that at an Episcopal church like St. Paul's where we were, it was a churchyard, not a cemetery. It seems churchyard is used whenever the burial place adjoins the sanctuary. I have been careful ever since because of what happened a few years after her passing. St. Paul's is governed by the Holy Trinity Church in Clemson, and the group in charge of St. Paul's decided a brick walkway must be constructed from the entrance to the churchyard back to Thomas Clemson's burial site. Mrs. John C. Calhoun and other family members are interred there, too. Though a fair-sized monument is in sight, maybe it would have taken some effort to get back there. My question, however, involves the walkway. Does it mean those buried on the far side of the walkway are in a cemetery and not a churchyard? I know it's picky, but I have wondered.

The church itself was erected in 1822 and has a lot of original furnishings inside. An 1848 George Jardine organ, originally hand-pumped, is a special feature. Mrs. John C. Calhoun led a drive to raise $300 for the purchase of the organ in New York. Mrs. Calhoun said the organ was necessary because no one liked the way the music leader "hissed" the words. The impressive windows were hand-blown glass and with breakage in the 1860s the panes were patched and remained until just a few years ago when the leaders of the church had them broken out and replaced with store-bought panes. It's still an impressive church and is not used for regular services.

Back to the delightful lady who corrected me; she cared for the church her entire adult life and had hired two different people to prepare her burial spot, in case one of them had died before her. She loved Pendleton, that's for sure. She said there was a rock on the village green that if stepped on meant you would never leave Pendleton. She also enjoyed standing on the side of the street and waving her cane at automobiles as they went by, saying cars should never have been allowed in town.

The first congregation for Pendleton was the Stone Meeting House, or Old Stone Church, and it was several miles out of town. It was built from 1797 to 1802 after a log church named Hopewell-on-the-Keowee burned in a forest fire. General Andrew Pickens had established it. A Presbyterian church, the congregation moved into Pendleton itself in the 1830s. No longer used as a house of worship, the self-perpetuating Old Stone Church and Cemetery Commission has carefully maintained it, and the cemetery (yes, that's the right word for Presbyterian burial places) has been expanded several times. Many founders of the region are buried there and some are mentioned in other stories.

Two interesting burials bear attention here. One is Robert Anderson, for whom the city and county are named. He established

St. Paul's Episcopal Church in Pendleton was organized in 1819 and this structure
was completed in 1822. The adjoining churchyard has the remains of many notables.
Photo by the author.

a plantation on the west side of the Seneca River and, as one of the founders of the Old Stone Church, stated his desire to be buried there. When he died, several days of rain had caused the river to rise too much and he had to be buried on his plantation. In the 1960s Lake Hartwell was being constructed and because the water would cover his burial site, his remains were removed to the church—again because of the water. His wish was finally granted.

The other unusual burial involved politics. In 1832, nullification was a big issue and the Pendleton people favored it to a great extent, as their neighbor John C. Calhoun was an absolute leader on public thought, strongly advocating the state to nullify any act of Congress injurious to the interests of the state. Benjamin F. Perry, a Greenville newspaper publisher who would later become governor, dared to oppose Calhoun's beliefs. Opponents of Perry brought in an out-of-state newspaperman, Turner Bynum, to start a paper and fight Perry in print. It got out of hand and a duel was proposed, which took

Carmel Presbyterian Church near the southern edge of Pickens County near Easley dates to the 1780s and actually is older than Old Stone Church. *Photo by the author.*

place on the Savannah River between South Carolina and Georgia. Bynum was killed and his remains were taken to the Stone Meeting House in a pouring rain. The church fathers would not let him be buried in the cemetery because of the way he died but offered space at the edge. Two pine saplings were used to carry him there, then stuck in the ground at either end of the grave. Cemeteries have a way of expanding. The Bynum grave now is almost in the center and the stumps of the trees are visible.

The church and cemetery are behind a low stone wall on U.S. 76 between Clemson and Pendleton, and loving care is taken care of the grounds. You may wish to stroll through and look at the stones, and maybe wonder why one is just a pile of rocks. It was the burial place of a Cherokee Indian. Elsewhere, there's no stone yet, and we hope it will be many years before it is used, but you'll find my wife and I there eventually. If there is a stone, stop and say hello.

Let's not forget the Pendleton Woolen Mills. We took great delight when tourists would come into the office and ask how to get to the woolen mills or outlet. With a smile, we would tell them to go west to California and turn north to Oregon. Oh, yes, there's the other Pendleton—the Pendleton District Historical, Recreational and Tourism Commission. It serves the entire Old Pendleton District— Anderson, Oconee and Pickens Counties—and is now involved with the South Carolina Heritage Corridor.

The Pendleton Farmers Society

I'm a city boy and always have been. In my Anderson newspaper days I was given the assignment of producing a farm page every Monday. It was almost like asking me to go take a picture of a farmer's jersey cows, and I would look for creatures wearing a jersey, most likely with CLEMSON printed on it. (Nothing personal. Tigers, I'm on your side.)

When I learned the Pendleton District Commission was looking for a director I assigned myself to attend the annual picnic of the Pendleton Farmers Society and spoke to the president, who was on the commission's board. I said I wanted the job. I got it and it lasted for thirty-six years. In the 1980s I was asked to become secretary-treasurer of the Society. It had nothing to do with my earlier farm page work; it was because my office was across from the other end of the village green where the Farmers Hall is located and I had a typewriter and a telephone. This was to be a non-paying job as a volunteer, and to this day I'm still at it.

As an organization, the Society was primarily an adult school for farmers—a pioneer in opening new and true methods of the "first and greatest vocation of man." Soil conservation in the early years

The landmark Pendleton Farmers Society has been in use since 1828. *Photo by the author.*

had been a major topic and one member said the two greatest things ever confronting him were how to make good and useful citizens of his children and how to keep his soil from washing away.

The Farmers Hall itself is one of the most notable landmarks of the Upstate and has been on the village green since 1828. The Society had its beginning in 1815, and when the state legislature divided the Pendleton District into Anderson and Pickens Districts, the Society bought the new courthouse that was under construction, completed it and has been meeting there ever since The second floor has always been the meeting hall and the ground floor has had a number of different tenants. It has been the post office, a millinery shop, an arts and crafts shop, a print shop and for many years now it has been a restaurant. The Society is the third oldest in the United States (Philadelphia and Charleston societies are older) and the Hall itself is the oldest in continuous use.

In the early years the Society met at least quarterly and also visited farms to study methods in use. There were also annual stock competitions, replaced in modern times by county fairs. Now the Society is primarily a social organization, having a spring business meeting and a fall family picnic on the village green, with the Hall close by in the event of rain. The spring meeting does have a speaker, generally on an agricultural topic. One year the speaker was Georgia peanut farmer Jimmy Carter, and he told members he would be announcing his candidacy for U.S. president in a few days. He did, was elected and you know the rest of the story. There is no speaker at the picnic.

Many Lowcountry planters and politicians had summer homes in and around Pendleton. Thomas Pinckney, who had been governor of South Carolina, had such a home at the edge of Pendleton and he became the first president of the Society in 1815. Certainly the most notable member was John C. Calhoun, who served as president in 1839. An avid farmer and even greater statesman, Calhoun's plantation was Fort Hill, now the center of the Clemson University campus. At the time, his mailing address was "Pendleton Court House."

Fort Hill on the Clemson University campus was the home of John C. Calhoun and the university's founder, Thomas Green Clemson. *Photo by the author.*

Calhoun's son-in-law, Thomas Green Clemson, acquired Fort Hill after Calhoun's death. In 1868 he became president of the Society. A vocal advocate for having an agricultural college in South Carolina, his words generally fell on deaf ears. (The argument was that South Carolina already had a college in Columbia and didn't need another one.) He resigned from the Society and tried again in 1874 on the college matter without luck. He decided to get even; when he died in 1888, his will stipulated that the Fort Hill plantation and a sum of money should go to the establishment of the college. It took a year of court battles and dissentions, but it finally passed by one vote. The end result is Clemson University.

A sundial stands near the entrance to the Hall. It was given to the Society by its owner, Colonel Francis K. Huger, on returning

A sundial with a unique past is on Pendleton's village green. *Photo by the author.*

This cannon played a hand in the election of Wade Hampton, governor of South Carolina in 1876. *Photo by the author.*

to Charleston from his summer home in Pendleton. It was given to Huger by the Marquis de Lafayette for Huger's attempt to rescue him from an Austrian prison, where he had been placed due to his political leanings. Huger was a medical student at the time, and when he failed in the rescue attempt he was imprisoned for some time. Lafayette stayed for several years and after his release he gave the sundial to Huger. (I don't know exactly how it works, but it looks historically nice there.)

Another artifact on the grounds near the Hall's entrance is a cannon. It had been presented to the town in 1861 by Theodore Wagoner, a Charleston merchant with a summer home in Pendleton, who had used it as a distress signal on one of his ships. It was used in the 1870s in Wade Hampton's successful campaign for governor. Pendleton men constructed a gun carriage and, like some others in the state, donned red shirts to help in the campaign. (I've never seen the newspaper, but tradition insists that when the Pendleton men rode into Anderson for a political rally, the headline read: "The streets were full of red shirts, the atmosphere was full of dust and the woods were full of Republicans.")

The cannon was supposedly put to rest on the village green as part of a red shirt reunion in 1906, but it wasn't permanent. Furman University once was all but in the downtown area of Greenville, and in 1951 the cannon was spirited away by some Clemson cadets, taken to the Furman campus and fired with blanks during the middle of the night. The sound was heard from blocks around and shattered glass in the Furman windows. There were reports the cadets used it on other occasions. It now is anchored in concrete.

Membership in the Farmers Society is made up of farmers, agricultural professors, farm-related public and private farm organizations and, most importantly, students who will be the future of the Society. Belonging to those groups or just being a descendant of a member is all that is required for membership, but a member must recommend the applicant. There were members from fifty-three South Carolina cities and towns and five other states at the most recent count.

Would There Be a Texas Without Pendleton?

*J*ames Butler Bonham was a close friend of William Travis and both were natives of the Saluda, South Carolina area. When Travis went to the Texas territory and became commander of troops at the Alamo, he had Bonham as his second in command. When trouble began brewing in Texas, Travis had written Bonham and urged him to come. At the time, Bonham was a resident of Pendleton and had his law office in town. He went posthaste.

Thomas Jefferson Rusk was a native of Pendleton; his father had been the builder of the Old Stone Church in 1797. Rusk became a lawyer and, with John C. Calhoun and others, invested in gold mines in Dahlonega, Georgia. Trusting his two managers, he visited the mines one day and discovered they had skipped town with the gold. Rusk took after them, finally finding them in Texas, where they had gambled all the money away. By this time, Rusk was almost penniless himself, and he stayed there where he later became a friend of Sam Houston. He assisted Houston throughout the campaigns with the Mexicans and became one of two Pendleton natives who became a signer of the declaration of independence for the Republic of Texas.

A wealthy Charlestonian went to Pendleton in 1800, liked the area and stayed there, buying up land everywhere he could while

The State of Texas erected this monument at Old Stone Church in memory of John and Mary Rusk, parents of Thomas Jefferson Rusk. John Rusk was the builder of the church. *Photo by the author.*

also becoming a major farmer and cattleman. His son, born in Pendleton, did not want to be a farmer or cattleman, so he went to Yale and obtained a law degree. Returning to Pendleton, he did not like the politics of the time so he struck out for Texas. He settled in San Antonio, where his son became the first white child born there. He set up his law practice while getting into politics, and as was the custom in those days, people would pay him with produce and sometimes a cow or a calf. Still not wanting to be a cattleman, he let the animals roam unbranded. People who saw an unbranded cow knew whose it was, saying, "That is a Maverick cow," meaning Samuel Augustus Maverick of Pendleton, South Carolina.

James Hamilton of Pendleton was a governor of South Carolina. When his term ended, he left for Texas and became the first ambassador to Europe for the new republic.

Barnard Bee Sr. moved his family to Pendleton from Goose Creek, near Charleston. While the family remained, Bee was always running off to the new Texas republic to assist the new government in every way he could—sometimes to the distress of those in the government. He became the first secretary of war and later secretary of the treasury and also held other offices in the early days. A son, Hamilton P. Bee, had gone to Texas with him on one trip, stayed and became involved in the early legislature. He eventually became a brigadier general during the Civil War, limiting his services to western campaigns.

John C. Calhoun was secretary of war when the United States went to war with Mexico, and he was vice president of the United States when he helped annex the Republic of Texas into the Union.

There are counties in Texas named for Bee, Calhoun, Hamilton, Maverick and Rusk, and there is an Anderson County named by people who moved from Anderson County, South Carolina, of which Pendleton is a part.

And how about the Texas county of Stonewall? How does it figure into the Pendleton connection? Barnard Bee had another son, Barnard Elliott Bee, who went to West Point from Pendleton and distinguished himself in the U.S. Army, resigning when the Civil War began. He became a brigadier general in the Confederate army and at the first battle of Manassas in an attempt to rally the troops, he saw Thomas Jonathan Jackson on horseback in the distance. Bee yelled out, "There stands Jackson like a stone wall! Rally around the Virginians!" Bee was mortally wounded moments later, but the name Stonewall is still with us.

Andersonville

An island is at the point where the Tugaloo and Seneca Rivers join to form the Savannah River. More than two hundred years ago, there was access by road and ferry and it was a favorite stopping place between Pendleton and Marthasville, Georgia.

In 1801 the South Carolina legislature created a town on the river, naming it for Revolutionary Colonel and later General Robert Anderson. Today, traces of the town can only be found by boat. It became an island when Lake Hartwell was created, and the lake didn't cover the high ground. Pendleton is still here and Marthasville has a new name—Atlanta.

The town served as a central point for river traffic, with goods coming and going between Andersonville and Hamburg (gone long before Lake Russell covered the site) and Augusta and Savannah, Georgia. There was a forty-room hotel, an iron foundry, cotton gin, sawmill, gristmill, gun factory, stables, cotton and wool factories and a thriving clock industry.

Samuel Earle, a prosperous Revolutionary War veteran, founded the town, which owed its principal success to its barge line and the extensive trade in cotton and animal skins. Earle, along with Baylis Earle and Robert Anderson, had been appointed commissioner to lay out the town, and the name was given to honor the man who later would have the county and city of Anderson carrying his name.

A female academy was established, merchants opened more stores and homes were quick to rise in the vicinity. It was on the brink of becoming a major town in South Carolina's Upcountry. Pendleton was virtually the only other town of size in the region, and while it continued as the courthouse seat for the Pendleton District, Andersonville was gaining in size. Even after Anderson District came into being and the courthouse town of Anderson was created, Andersonville continued to thrive. Iron and water would be its downfall.

In 1840 heavy flooding on the Tugaloo and Seneca Rivers destroyed the cotton and woolen mills, along with many other businesses and homes. Rebuilding began, and the town continued to hold on. In 1852 another flood wiped much of the town away, and it was never rebuilt. Colonel Frank Harrison saw a potential for the town in the 1850s. The Columbia and Greenville Railroad—the iron horse—was being constructed into Anderson and would handle the goods barges had earlier shipped, and he promoted a line on to Andersonville as being a spark to rejuvenate the dying community. It never came.

A few families continued to live there, and a post office was maintained until 1893. Andersonville Baptist Church remained at the site for many years. While almost a ghost town after World War II, Andersonville's fate was sealed in the 1960s. Lake Hartwell began filling and covered all but the high ground. Today, the foundations of a few buildings can be found, and Andersonville sits as a dim reminder of a glorious past. There have been discussions over the years to develop a park there, and while the U.S. Army Corps of Engineers, South Carolina Department of Parks, Recreation and Tourism and Anderson County have discussed plans, none have been advanced.

One thing is for certain with Andersonville, however. It is *not* the site of the infamous Andersonville Prison during and after the War Between the States. The distinction goes to an area in south Georgia, near Americus—in spite of what some people may have read in books and brochures.

Do You Believe?

My LPOE, or Late Place of Employment, was located in Pendleton's Hunters Store, an 1850 two-story brick structure that did not have electricity or plumbing until 1968 (not that it has anything to do with this story).

I was staying after business hours to work on a small upstairs museum (which no longer exists) when I heard the downstairs door open and close. Thinking it was an employee who had returned for some reason or another, I called down the stairs and, receiving no reply, I went down the worn stairs to investigate and found no one. Then, I heard footsteps upstairs and returning, found no one. I called home and asked if supper had been prepared and being told it had not, I asked them to hold off a short while, as I was coming home.

Since that time, probably in the early 1970s, the resident ghost has been heard and even seen a number of times by others. One employee heard him (and we did know it was a him) and saw him at the foot of the stairs. She described him, saying he was curly-headed and had on a black suit. When she turned to look at him fully, he was no longer there. Frequently we would hear boxes being dropped, along with other noises. When investigated, nothing was out of order. One time we placed the office chairs in certain positions at closing time, and they had been moved when we returned the next day.

The 1850 Hunters Store has a resident ghost. *Photo by the author.*

Years after the first sighting, another employee rounded the counter to get water from the fountain, and she gasped and turned pale. The curly-headed, black-suited person was standing in the corner. She later told this story to a gathering and one of the persons there, who had been a volunteer at the office years earlier, told her she had seen him dressed the same way but would say nothing, fearing people would think she was crazy. Our grandson, who would have been about three at the time, came into my office to say there was a man outside. When investigated, there was no one, but the grandson claimed he was standing at almost the same spot he had been viewed earlier and he was curly-headed and wore a black suit.

Fine researchers that we were, we never pursued the matter, and it took a then high school student interviewing one of the former owners of the store to get the story. It seems that, according to the late B.G. "Punch" Hunter, a Pendleton resident astride his horse fell into a nearby stream. He was already soaked on the inside and the stream certainly drenched his outer person. He was brought to the Hunters Store to dry out and sober up in a one-room apartment located on the second floor for the store's caretaker. It was in May and the windows were open, but it turned cold and the man, whose name was known but not identified because of descendants still living in the town, died from the exposure.

On one occasion, I was assisting two female tourists at the counter, and one of them started shuddering and said, "There is something here." They started to leave and her companion stated, "She is a psychic." Another time it was necessary for the entire staff to leave, and a friend was asked to stay as he had work to do on the computer. He was told not to bother answering the phone. After it rang several times, it obviously disturbed the resident tenant as he started running up and down the upstairs, knocking items over as he went. Of course, when the area was checked, nothing had been disturbed.

Written in pencil on the door frame at the one-room apartment, which Punch Hunter remembered being there but not knowing who did it, were these words: "May 1984. Cold. May 29, 1896. Very Cold."

Ready for another one?

There is a historic home in Pendleton (one of many, so don't try to figure it out) that had been purchased by out-of-town people who hired a caretaker to live in it for several months until they could move. Asleep one night, he heard something and looked at the end of the bed. Standing there was a man in overalls who disappeared when the caretaker bolted up.

Another time he heard something again, and the same man was there with a cup of coffee in his hand. He turned to leave, and the caretaker slowly got up to follow him. He saw the man walk through the wall and disappear. The house, built in the 1840s, originally had the entrance on the side of the house where the specter disappeared, but was moved in the early 1900s to another location, and the door was replaced by a wall.

Okay, one more?

It's one of my favorites and took place in Oconee County. For many years I would do a slide show (I think they call them audiovisual presentations or Power Point presentations now) at Oconee State Park during the summer for the campers and cabin users, showing them places they could visit when they wished to explore the region. After several years of that, someone proposed that ghost stories be told like the ones I have been discussing. Everyone gathered on the long front porch of the former main building to hear the stories, and families stretched out the entire length. When the lights came back on, there was just a tightly knit group in the center.

The wonderful state park is on South Carolina Highway 107 and just up the road is a pull-off called Moody Springs. On the mountain near that site an airplane had crashed in the 1940s, and the pilot was never found. Since then, strange things have happened! On a dark and rainy night (naturally), persons traveling that road have seen someone walking on the side of the road. Some have picked him up, including two ministers at different times, and the generally silent passenger always asked to be let out at the overlook on South Carolina 28 from (and into, of course) Walhalla. On letting him out, he was not seen again. Other times on the same kind of night, he would be heading the other direction and always asked to be let out at Moody Springs, where he disappeared.

Could it be the pilot who was destined to always remain on the mountain? You decide. I do know what our two children think. My daughter was a teenager at the time and my son was seven years younger. On the famous dark and rainy night, we were leaving the state park after the usual Tuesday storytelling. We saw a man in a black raincoat walking down the highway and I said I would pick him up. My daughter, who often told ghost stories along with me, started screaming. My brave son not only dropped to the floor in the back, but also tried to crawl under the seat.

The Name Game

Place names come in many forms, some for notable people, some for locations and some just plain unusual. Take Fair Play, for example. It seems a fight broke out at a store there and the onlookers started yelling "fair play." The town's in Oconee County.

Other Oconee names include Walhalla, named by the German Colonization Society that settled the town in 1850 and decided it was "Valhalla," the garden of the gods. Seneca is named for the Indian tribe that was in the area but not at that site. West Union is named for a temperance union that was west of another temperance union. A community in the county is named South Union because it was south of—well, you know. Westminster is named for the church in England. The community of Mountain Rest is just that, and it's nice.

Pickens County, which preceded Oconee as a part of the Pendleton District and then the Pickens District, became a county in 1868. It is named for the Revolutionary War General Andrew Pickens, as is the courthouse town. Easley is named for William King Easley, and Clemson is named for Thomas Green Clemson, founder of Clemson College, now Clemson University. A town adjoining the school was Calhoun, named for Clemson's father-in-law, and earlier the entire area had been named Fort Hill, Calhoun's home place. Dacusville is named for an early settler.

Woodburn, now a house museum in Pendleton, has four stories and twenty-two rooms. It is on U.S. Highway 76. *Photo by the author.*

Six Mile is so named because the town is six miles from the Cherokee town of Keowee. Liberty's name has several suggestions, but the most popular is that it grew out of Salubrity, a stage stop there. (A friend, some years ago when hitchhiking was popular particularly for Clemson cadets, recalled one Sunday evening leaving home in Greenville. He got as far as quiet, small Liberty just after dark and started yelling out, "If this is Liberty, give me death!" He was late for class on Monday because police heard him and he spent the night in jail.) Central is so-named because it is the railroad midway point between Atlanta and Charlotte.

Anderson city and county are named for Colonel Robert Anderson, as told elsewhere in this volume. Belton is named for Judge Belton O'Neal, a railroad official who sparked the railroad coming there. Iva is named for the daughter of a Doctor Bryson who lived there. Nearby Starr was named for a popular railroad engineer. Pendleton's name is for Judge Henry Pendleton, and that story is detailed elsewhere. The textile town of Pelzer is named for Francis J. Pelzer, who founded four textile plants there. Piedmont, a geographic term, had the first textile plants, one in Anderson County and the other across the Saluda River in Greenville County—both long gone now. Townville is a fanciful name, as is Sandy Springs.

This isn't a town name, but a story worth telling because it involves a community. The late Mrs. Jane Milam of Sandy Springs wrote a little volume about the community and told about the campground meetings. Families living nearby would come for the day and, after arriving, would often leave a baby in the wagon to sleep. While services extended into the evening, the young Sandy Springs boys would often take a baby from one wagon and put it in another. The family, heading home late at night, would not pay attention to the baby until they reached to get him from the wagon on arrival at home. Mrs. Milam said it sometimes took days to get the right baby back to the right house.

A Tunnel to Nowhere

The dream to have a railroad from Charleston, South Carolina, to Cincinnati, Ohio, in the 1850s dissolved in the mountains of present-day Oconee County—or rather, it ran up against a granite wall.

A direct line to the Midwest for provisions and passengers was the idea of the Blue Ridge Railroad Company. For South Carolinians, any people or materials coming from the Midwest had to go to New York, and then go south by ship to Charleston, the premier city at the time. The rail line was completed to Anderson, Pendleton and West Union by the late 1850s, but the solid granite Stumphouse Mountain was to be the stumbling block. Before the rail company could recoup, the nation was divided and had gone to war.

A contract had been awarded for work starting in 1856 on three tunnels in South Carolina, all in the mountains near Walhalla. A town, Tunnel Hill, was begun atop Stumphouse Mountain and hundreds of workers were brought in. Mostly Irish immigrants, they labored twelve hours a day, six days a week with only sledgehammers, hand drills and black powder for blasting purposes. The town had a Catholic church and more than a dozen saloons, which likely kept the workers happy.

Saddle Tunnel was to have been 616 feet long and 200 feet were completed before work was halted. Middle Tunnel was 385 feet long,

Stumphouse Tunnel Park above Walhalla is a cool place to be in the summertime, and the temperature doesn't change in the winter! *Photo by the author.*

and though completed, rock slides long ago sealed it up. The longest tunnel in the system was to have been Stumphouse Tunnel, so named because of a large hollowed-out tree at the site that had been made into a dwelling. (Really!) It would have been 5,863 feet in length. The tunnel level was 236 feet below the highest point of the mountain, and by 1857 all work was concentrated on Stumphouse. Four vertical shafts were dug to provide ventilation, allowing workers to cut from the four bases.

At peak manpower, workers were able to chip away two hundred feet a month. Crews started at either end of the tunnel route and other crews created the shafts and, on reaching the base, began cutting toward the other crews to connect with each other. Only in one case was this engineering feat accomplished. Workers from the end, which is open to the public, connected with the crew cutting from the first shaft. Visitors can see, by looking closely at the walls and observing the angle of the cuts, just where the two crews connected. Considering that this was done in the dark with only a candle in a helmet with no way of knowing just where the other crew was, the connection was right on the mark.

The number one shaft, rising 161 feet, is unique. Due to the mixture of air from the outside and the fifty-degree coolness of the tunnel itself, it is always raining—not moisture, but actual rain. Crews were able to cut 1,600 feet from the opening before funds ran out in 1859, and war was on the horizon. None of the other sections were ever connected, and the far end of the tunnel, which is open, is underwater. The other two tunnels are sealed for safety's sake.

The South was in no position to resume construction after the Civil War, and the tunnel remains uncompleted as a memorial to engineering. The town is gone, except for a graveyard barely marked with unlettered granite from the tunnel. Some of that same granite was used in more modern times to erect buildings at Tamassee DAR School, and for bridge and church construction.

Stumphouse Tunnel Park is on South Carolina Highway 28 north of Walhalla and was developed by the Pendleton District Historical, Recreational and Tourism Commission. It now is owned and operated very well by the town of Walhalla and it is on the National Register of Historic Places.

As an addendum, a few things must be clarified. Many people have heard the tunnel has eyeless snakes as inhabitants. *No way!* Union sympathizers hid in the tunnel during the Civil War. *Possible, but no proof.* Blue cheese was manufactured in the tunnel. *Yes!* Clemson College used it in the 1950s as the temperature was just right and a brick wall denotes where it was located. Clemson now makes the cheese in a modern building on campus.

Who's On First?

Every town, city, county, state and nation has "firsts" of some kind or another. Let's see what the old tri-county Pendleton District of South Carolina can claim:

Francis Salvador, an Englishman of the Jewish faith, came to South Carolina prior to the American Revolution and was a member of the First and Second Provincial Congresses. He was aide-de-camp to Major Andrew Williamson in the campaign against the Cherokee Indians and Loyalists and in the first battle on August 1, 1776, at the Cherokee town of Seneca, now a part of the Clemson University campus, he was mortally wounded. There are statues and plaques memorializing him in London and Charleston, as he was the first person of the Jewish faith to die for America.

In 1894 William C. Whitner of Anderson found a way to transmit electricity over a line, making Anderson the first town in the South to have transmitted electricity. Anderson Cotton Mill became the first to be operated by electricity from lines over a distance, and Oliver Bolt's cotton gin was the first to be powered by electricity. Anderson is still known as the Electric City.

Dr. Leda Bruce Hurst of Anderson was the first woman to pass the South Carolina dentistry examination in 1919.

The "Ripley Bridge" is on U.S. Highway 76 in Anderson County between Sandy Springs and LaFrance. It was in *Ripley's Believe It Or Not* as all forms of traffic are at the one spot—highway, railroad, waterway over Three and Twenty Creek and a footpath. A commercial photographer once pasted an airplane in the sky to represent air traffic! *Photo by the author.*

The first recorded aviation death in South Carolina occurred on November 2, 1905, at Buena Vista Park in Anderson. As part of the Riddle-Southern Carnival, hot air balloonist Maude Broadwick fell from the ascending balloon as spectators watched.

The first group of delegates to fly to a convention was members of the Anderson Lions Club, going to a convention in 1926 in Orangeburg. A member's friend had to land his rickety, dinosaurian Sikorsky airplane in Anderson for unplanned repairs. It was the largest commercial craft in the United States at the time and the pilot offered to fly the Andersonians to the convention. Fourteen men made the trip; ten chose to return by automobile.

Margaret McCollum Lever was the first female student at Clemson College in 1932. Due to the Depression, financially strapped faculty members were allowed to enroll daughters at Clemson rather than sending them to Winthrop. Clemson was a military, agricultural and

Hagood Mill, on U.S. Highway 178 north of Pickens, was built in the early 1800s. Restored, it now has several outbuildings associated with the area and is operated by Pickens County. *Photo by the author.*

mechanical college at the time. Margaret Marie Snider Coker was the first coed graduate, however, in the class of 1957, women having been admitted in the 1954–55 school year.

The first African American to be admitted to Clemson was Harvey Gantt on January 23, 1963, as an architectural student. He later became mayor of Charlotte, North Carolina.

The first American woman to be pictured on paper money— a Confederate $100 bill—was Lucy Holcombe Pickens, wife of Governor Francis W. Pickens, a native of Pendleton and grandson of Revolutionary General Andrew Pickens.

Pickens County was the first in South Carolina to conduct a Democratic primary on August 18, 1876. Prior to that time, delegates made all nominations for political office to conventions. The county was among the first to vote Republican in modern times.

Francis Burt of Pendleton was the first governor of the Nebraska Territory, being appointed in 1953 by President Franklin Pierce. He died on a stagecoach en route to the territory, and while he never served, his portrait hangs in the state capitol in Lincoln.

Newberry College was first in Walhalla, where it was known as Adger College. The name was changed when the people of Newberry offered space for the Lutheran school.

Lander College in Greenwood was first in Williamston. It was founded by the Reverend William Lander as the Williamston Female Seminary and was named in his honor when it was moved.

Dr. William B. Johnson of Anderson, head of Johnson Female Seminary, was the founder and first president of the South Carolina Baptist Convention, and he was the first president of the Southern Baptist Convention.

Jesse Cornelius Stribling of Pendleton had the first registered herd of Jersey cattle in South Carolina and one of the first in the Southeast (1873). He built the first silo in South Carolina (1881) and won top honors at the state fair.

John W. Stribling of Oconee and Anderson Counties invented the driving axle and differential gears (patented June 13, 1882) still used in today's automobiles and trucks. He fashioned the equipment to a steam engine and his carriage but never profited by the invention, as the automobile with a gas engine was only a few years in the future.

The Real Band of Brothers

Television, in recent years, had a popular series entitled *Band Of Brothers*, dealing with a unit in World War II. It can't be confused with this story, however, because this deals with real brothers and, primarily, the Civil War. It started like this:

In my newspaper days in 1961, I produced an entire year's worth of articles on the Civil War and stumbled across three brothers of Pendleton whose story had never been told. As I toured many of the war's hallowed sites, I started gathering information on them. When I left the newspaper business to go to Pendleton, stories on the change commented that I was finishing a manuscript on these brothers.

Thirty-six years later, when I retired, articles stated that I was finishing a manuscript on the same three brothers. Lazy? No, those thirty-six years required dealing with other facets of history and tourism. I had, however, secured a national grant to complete my studies, and the mostly finished manuscript just sat there on the computer, but in a format that was not compatible with any other computer. (So much for bargains!)

I used the material in many of my talks, and on one occasion when I had finished, a man came up to me and said, "Quit talking and get back to writing." So I did, and here is a condensed version of what it's all about:

Clement Hoffman Stevens. *Courtesy of the Caroliniana Society, Columbia.*

Henry Kennedy Stevens. *Courtesy of the Caroliniana Society, Columbia.*

Peter Fayssoux Stevens. *Courtesy of the Caroliniana Society, Columbia.*

Clement William Stevens could point to a varied and interesting life. Just how many people could look back to starting life in Jamaica, being reared for a while in Charleston, then going to sea and fighting pirates and becoming an officer before finally settling in Florida among the Indians with a wife and young family—at still just over thirty years old. He went to sea when he was fifteen and was at sea at the outbreak of the War of 1812 with England. He survived the war and was with Stephen Decatur in battles with Barbary pirates. He saw other sea duty and was permitted to go to Charleston in 1820.

Stevens was there to marry Sarah Johnston Fayssoux, youngest daughter of Dr. Peter Fayssoux, chief physician and surgeon of the Southern department during the American Revolution. Sarah was particularly close to an older sister, Ann Wragg Fayssoux, who had married Barnard Bee of Goose Creek near Charleston and was spending her time in Charleston and Pendleton, where the Bees had moved. The bride and groom went on to Norwich, Connecticut, where Clement was next assigned. It was there, on August 14, 1821, that Sarah gave birth to Clement Hoffman Stevens. A daughter, Helen Fayssoux Stevens, followed in 1822.

Perhaps it was a growing family as well as seeing family members succeeding with Florida sugar cane plantations that caused Stevens to resign his commission and purchase property not far from Tallahassee on a road leading to other plantations, including one owned by James Gadsden of Charleston. Stevens named his plantation Chapofo for unknown reasons. Clement and Sarah started raising cane and started raising more children. Young Clement and Helen soon had more siblings. Henry Kennedy Stevens was born in 1824, Ann Fayssoux Stevens was born in 1826, James Gadsden Stevens was born in 1827 and Martha Stevens followed in 1829. Peter Fayssoux Stevens came next, followed by Barnard Bee Stevens and Mary Elizabeth Stevens.

As the children were growing, so was unrest with the Seminole Indians. Gadsden was appointed commissioner to negotiate a treaty in 1832, which would move the Indians west of the Mississippi River and open the Florida land to white settlers. While some tribes made the move, the Seminoles rebelled. The proposed new Indian land would adjoin the Creek Indians', and already Creeks were capturing Seminoles as well as their allies, runaway blacks, and making both of them slaves. The Stevens family letters relate how Seminoles frequently passed through Chapofo and were mainly friendly. Then a new Seminole leader, Osceola, had gathered forces and was harassing army troops, and in 1835 the Seminoles killed an entire company of soldiers, including its commanding officer.

Plantation owners grouped together in forts as much as they could for protection, and as the situation worsened it was decided that women and children should be removed. Clement William Stevens helped load his family into wagons. His wife and children headed for Pendleton to take refuge with her sister, Ann Bee. The Seminoles continued on a rampage. The family never saw or heard from Clement William Stevens again.

Sarah Stevens, when she arrived Pendleton in 1835 with her brood, certainly could see the Charleston influence she had known so well from her childhood days. She was even more secure since she was with her sister and her family, the Barnard Bees, formerly from Charleston and now settled in their permanent home. Colonel Bee was a son of Thomas Bee, a member of South Carolina's Council of Safety prior to the American Revolution.

It was a crowded household for a while. The Bees had their own family, including sons Barnard and Hamilton and daughters Susan, Ann, Mattie, Emma and Marie. In 1833 Colonel Bee had purchased the home of former South Carolina Governor James Hamilton and named it, logically, the Bee Hive. The family had lived in a smaller place in the heart of town before that time. Hamilton, a family friend, had been mayor of Charleston, was in the state legislature, served several times in Congress and was governor in 1830, taking an active part in opposition to tariff duties and supporting the idea of nullification along with the man he most admired, John C. Calhoun. Hamilton Bee was named for him.

Sarah's oldest, Clement Hoffman Stevens, or "Clem" as the family called him, was at age fourteen pretty much the male head of the household. He stayed in Pendleton only a short time, however, as his education—limited mostly to what his parents had taught him—was to come at sea, although not as a sailor.

Here was a forty-year-old mother, not yet knowing the fate of her husband in Florida. Settling in was a slow process, as the refuge was expected to be a short one, and Chapofo, Florida, continued for some time to be listed as the home of the family. Helen, in 1835, was thirteen and her mother's right arm. Henry Kennedy, often called "Hal" or "Harry," was eleven. Ann was nine; James, eight; Martha, six; Peter Fayssoux, sometimes called "Pete" and more often "Fayssoux," was five; Barnard was three; and Mary was one year old.

John C. Calhoun, a native of Abbeville, which neighbored the Pendleton District, had moved to the district in 1824, acquiring and enlarging a house he named Fort Hill. It was on high ground overlooking the site of Fort Rutledge, established for a short time during the American Revolution as a base against the Cherokees. Calhoun had served in the state legislature, had been in Congress, served as secretary of war under President James Monroe and was vice president of the United States in Andrew Jackson's administration when he left Abbeville for Pendleton.

In 1832 Calhoun was in his second term as vice president. Protective tariffs had been established, altered and finally a compromise bill was entered that still made South Carolina angry. In a state convention, an ordinance declaring the act null and void was passed. The nullification declared the right to secede from the Union if the state should be challenged by force on the part of the federal government.

Antislavery had already been a major subject, and the question was often raised in connection with the tariff issue. Most of the states added to the nation after the American Revolution were slaveholding Southern states, and the matter of slavery did not sit well at all with the Northern industrializing areas. People were also beginning to take notice of Americans who had been settling a section of Mexico where they were calling themselves "Texans."

These were the issues on the minds and tongues of most everyone by the time Sarah Stevens and her children had come to South Carolina, and the Texans were certainly the topic at the Bee household, as the father, Colonel Barnard Bee, had already left for the territory. Others from the state, including many from Pendleton, were going or were already there. Bee had been a signer of the nullification ordinance in 1832 and now was offering his services in negotiations with the Mexican government.

In 1837 Colonel Bee's wife, son Hamilton and daughter Marie joined him in Texas. Marie died in the short time they were there and Ann Bee did not care for the territory and returned to Pendleton, leaving fifteen-year-old Hamilton with his father. Sarah Stevens remained in Pendleton with her children and the younger Bee children. Sarah had said her goodbyes to son Clem in 1836. Commodore William Shubrick and Captain Edward Shubrick of the United States Navy were related to the Bees, and Clem, now age fifteen, was given an appointment as captain's clerk. He sailed on several voyages into the West Indies and Brazil with both Shubricks in a civilian capacity, learning as he went.

The Bees were communicants at St. Paul's Episcopal Church in Pendleton, and Sarah Stevens and her children joined them. For that matter, most everyone in Pendleton with a Charleston connection was a member of the church. The Lowcountry people had established it in 1819. When they started moving in to escape the summer heat, the only other congregation was the Presbyterian church, founded by the Scots-Irish. Pendleton had not lost its influence, however. The Baptists and Methodists established churches later, and the Lowcountry people still migrated there in the summertime. Dave U. Sloan, recalling the town in the 1840s, remembered Pendleton had four flourishing churches and two hotels, a farmers' hall, schools and a secure peaceful population graced often by Calhoun's presence.

Sloan vividly remembered "magnificent coaches and the elegant spans of horses that whirled up the dust in the streets of the old town" and he wrote, "What old citizen's heart is not made to throb at the recollection of thrilling notes from the stage horn, borne over the hills to notify them of its coming? How the people would gather around the hotels and the post office as the great, ponderous vehicle came rolling and swaying over rocks, drawn by four or six horses, with its passengers and mail. And with what eager excitement the citizens sought to welcome friends and visitors, and receive the tardy news."

There may have been scenes like that when Sarah Stevens learned Seminole Indians led by Osceola had killed her husband and that Osceola was later captured and imprisoned at Fort Moultrie in Charleston Harbor. This was how she likely got the news that Colonel James Gadsden was administering Clement William Stevens's estate and would be guardian for the children.

Schooling was important for the children, and some of the choices were the Pendleton Male and Female Academies, ministers and their wives and a few spinsters. Records are not available listing the rolls of every year at the academies, but it was known Helen, Ann and Mary Elizabeth Stevens attended the Pendleton Female Academy, along with Mattie and Emma Bee. The boys, including cousin Barnard Elliott Bee, often called "Barnie," were at the male academy.

Dave U. Sloan recalled the male academy, located across the road from the Episcopal church, as a school "where the boys drilled daily, and wore gray uniforms and brass buttons." The female academy was located in the former jail, an impressive two-story building that had been completed just a few years before Pendleton lost its courthouse status. Sloan said it was where the young ladies were taught "etiquette and French, graceful attitudes, and 'highfalutin' notions,' modern manners, to walk daintily, and to scream fashionably at a bug or mouse."

By 1839 the Republic of Texas was well established but wanting to be annexed into the United States, and Colonel Bee was about to become minister to the United States to help with the negotiations. Hamilton Bee that year was placed on a commission to fix the boundary between Texas and the United States. Both father and son had come to Pendleton to visit family members for a while, and Colonel Bee wrote his friend Doctor Ashbel Smith that his wife was still lamenting the death of Marie, and he had observations about the education of his children who had stayed in Pendleton. Commenting on his fifteen-year-old namesake, he wrote: "My son, Barnard, and I scarcely knew, perhaps from his <u>formal</u> manner of <u>meeting</u> me…He is totally unlike Hamilton—brown with black eyes, intelligent enough, but without application."

Henry Kennedy Stevens was also fifteen years old in 1839, and Colonel Gadsden had secured him a commission on May 2 as a midshipman in the United States Navy. Hal was assigned to the *Macedonian*, carrying the same name as a frigate captured from the British in 1812. The earlier ship burned back in 1832, but the new one carried the figurehead bust of Alexander the Great that was salvaged from the fire. Kinsman Commodore Shubrick commanded the fleet.

James Gadsden Stevens and Martha Stevens died shortly after the Florida refugees came to Pendleton. Now with Hal gone, nine-year-old Pete Fayssoux was the ranking male member of the family at home. Clem remained at sea as a clerk, Hal was following in the wake of his father and young Barnie Bee's future had not been decided.

The people of Pendleton looked to their beloved neighbor, John C. Calhoun, for guidance. He was a good neighbor; a member of the Pendleton Farmers Society, active in agricultural matters, which were considered his first love, rather than politics; and a frequent visitor in town, present for most every social occasion when he was not in Washington. For the Stevens boys, as well as the Bees, likely in awe of the man who entertained some of the great people of the nation at his home and in town, the decade would bring dramatic changes to their lives.

AT HOME AND ABROAD

Colonel Barnard Bee's son Hamilton, who was born in Charleston in 1822, was happy with the political knowledge he was gathering in the new Republic of Texas. His brother, Barnard Elliott Bee, a Charlestonian born in 1824, was heading for a military life, and in 1841 he received an appointment to the United States Military Academy at West Point.

Barnie was named a "cadet-at-large," and while his residence was listed as Pendleton, his father was in Washington acting on behalf of the Republic of Texas. In 1843 Colonel Bee was recalled as minister to the United States, having not succeeded in getting recognition of Texas as a republic by antislavery England and France. Back in Pendleton, he wrote Dr. Ashbel Smith, the family had been pleased with a visit, saying, "He is greatly improved…he is not a student and therefore only ranks respectfully, tho very popular with the corps." Cadet Bee was certainly making himself known at West Point. On his third day he was cited as being "Absent from Parade" on the Fourth of July, and in his first month, he was reported for delinquencies six times and received the first of many demerits for "Tobacco in Possession." There was doubt that he would last the year.

He made it, however, even though he was regularly cited for swearing, inattention, absences, worn or dirty uniforms and gear, smoking, chewing and drinking. His freshman year, Bee finished 115th among 217 cadets—and it was his best year. The remaining three years, he ranked 192, 174 and 148 in a corps of some 210 cadets. Bee was popular with the cadets, showing the style of a Southern gentleman all the time. He was not considered unruly, but it was obvious he did not care to give up his lifestyle. French, infantry and artillery tactics did bring high grades, and when he graduated in 1845, he was thirty-third in a class of forty-one. Commissioned a second lieutenant, he was assigned to border patrol in the Republic of Texas.

In 1845 Henry Kennedy Stevens, twenty years old and a seasoned sailor, had been to the west coast of South America, the islands of the Pacific, San Francisco and had gone on to Brazil and the South American east coast. He had finished his apprenticeship in 1843 and had come ashore to Philadelphia to attend the asylum and pass his examination to be a passed midshipman. The asylum was the only naval school, other than classes provided aboard ships, which was available in the nation at the time, but two years later the government established an academy at Annapolis, Maryland. (I could make a funny about the navy and an asylum, but I'm an old salt myself and will leave it alone.)

There was a significant event that took place in Charleston in 1842. At that time, South Carolina had two arsenals, in Charleston and

Columbia, with troops on duty to protect the arms and munitions stored there. Governor John P. Richardson conceived the idea of removing the troops and turning the arsenals into schools, to be guarded by the students while they received an education. It marked the creation of the South Carolina Military Academy, housed in the Charleston arsenal known as The Citadel.

On January 1, 1846, at the age of fifteen, Peter Fayssoux Stevens left his home in Pendleton and was enrolled as a cadet at the military academy. His life in the quiet town of Pendleton, attending school and worshipping at St. Paul's Episcopal Church, had ended and a new world was opening up.

Clement Hoffman Stevens was leaving his sea duties and was aboard the USS *Saratoga* when brother Hal met him March 2, 1846, in Montevideo, Uruguay. On December 31, 1846, the brothers sailed into Norfolk, Virginia, together, having been on the sea for fifty-three days. Clem was in Charleston by 1847, the city where his father had spent younger days, and now he could frequently visit his younger brother, Fayssoux, as a cadet.

Annexation of Texas had become a major issue in the nation. Northern abolitionists opposed annexation for the very reason the South favored it—it would open up more territory where slavery was possible. In 1844 John Tyler was president of the United States and John C. Calhoun had left the Senate for an unsuccessful try at the presidency. He readily became secretary of state with the primary purpose of bringing Texas into the Union. Both sides agreed to terms of a treaty drawn up under Calhoun's hand, but the United States Senate rejected it, and Mexico continued to threaten war if it ever did happen. Compromises were worked out in 1845, with Congress finally agreeing to annexation. Young Barnard E. Bee would soon find himself in the middle of a war with Mexico. His brother Ham, by now secretary to the Texas Senate, resigned early in 1846 to join the Texas army.

War with Mexico included the Mexican California territory, and Navy Midshipman Henry Kennedy Stevens, no sooner than he had come back to the United States, found himself on the supply ship

Southampton on the West Coast in support of the American troops there. California was seized and claimed by the United States, and by the end of the year the war was concluding. During the year, in a battle at Cerro Gordo on April 18, 1846, Barnard E. Bee, now a first lieutenant, was severely wounded. He was cited for his "gallant and meritorious service" there. Recovering, he distinguished himself again on September 13 at Chapultepec and was promoted to captain. In appreciation, the state of South Carolina presented him with a commemorative sword, a beautifully designed piece that he was reluctant to list in his biography for West Point, not wanting to brag.

Hamilton Bee was discharged in October 1847 and went to Laredo to become a merchant. The following year, he married Maria Andrea Martinez, daughter of Don Andre Martinez Alcalde of Nuevo Laredo, Tamulipas, Mexico. She was fifteen years old, and Ham had met the family while assisting in the establishment of government in the Laredo area.

Clement Hoffman Stevens, regaining his land legs after more than ten years at sea, was establishing himself in Charleston in 1847. He had learned well in the company of naval leaders and other influential people of the time, and with their support and that of guardian James Gadsden, he had become a teller at the Planters and Mechanics Bank by 1848. The bank had been established in 1810 and unlike other banks at the time, which seemed to be content with commercial business in Charleston, the Planters and Mechanics Bank wanted to do just what the name said—serve the agricultural interests as well as the mechanical. It even had branches in other parts of the state, reaching out to the farmers, and proved to be one of the most successful banks in South Carolina during many years of operation. His financial knowledge quickly began to impress many people.

A twenty-six-year-old banker needed to show he was a solid, settled citizen, and on May 10, 1848, at the home of her parents in Pendleton, Clement married Ann Fayssoux Bee. As a young teenager when his family came from Florida to live with the Bees, it may well have been love at first sight. Ann was thirty years old. The newlyweds went back to Charleston and established a home, and in all likelihood were present at the South Carolina Military Academy in 1849 when Peter Fayssoux Stevens was graduated first in his class.

Fayssoux was appointed an assistant instructor in mathematics during his junior year, having studied under Francis Withers Capers, a graduate of the College of Charleston and a son of William Capers, who in 1846 had become the Methodist bishop of South Carolina. F.W. Capers left The Citadel in 1847 for a while, but would return. On August 17, 1849, Barnard E. Bee went home to Pendleton, and he and midshipman A.P. Warley of Pendleton were wined and dined by citizens of the town for their contributions during the Mexican War. Among those in attendance at a dinner were John C. Calhoun and South Carolina Governor W.B. Seabrook.

On March 31, 1850, John C. Calhoun died in Washington, fighting to the last for his beliefs in the South, as well as showing a love for the Union—in its proper place. In South Carolina, Calhoun's death at age sixty-eight brought a period of mourning that lasted a month. Tributes and plans for his funeral and burial filled the newspapers, as well as delicate bidding wars on just where he would be put to rest. The *Charleston Daily Courier* bordered lengthy articles in black; The Citadel Academy, in a resolution on April 1, called Calhoun's death a "national calamity" and said, "the Southern States (and particularly South Carolina) have suffered an irreparable loss." Virtually every town in the state passed resolutions. Columbia asked that he be buried there, it being the capital. Pendleton's resolution assumed he would be brought to Fort Hill, although he had never expressed a preference himself. Calhoun's sons agreed to a temporary burial in Charleston, with the right to have the remains moved elsewhere at a later date.

Charleston pulled out all the stops and prepared one of the most elaborate funerals known at the time. Literally thousands of people lined the streets as Calhoun's body finally got to Charleston on April 25, having already being laid in state in Washington; Richmond and Petersburg, Virginia; and Wilmington, North Carolina. A full page of details for the funeral, and the order in which various organizations would stand on the streets, was published. The funeral took place on the Citadel Square, and among the mourners was banker Clement Stevens, well remembering Calhoun as a friend at his wedding two years earlier in Pendleton. The statesman was buried at St. Philip's Episcopal Church the following day, and his remains are there today.

Just where Peter Fayssoux Stevens was at this time is not known, but on November 29, 1851, he was appointed lieutenant and professor at the Arsenal Academy in Columbia. The Arsenal Academy was a part of the South Carolina Military Academy, as established in 1842. On December 11, 1852, he was transferred to The Citadel in Charleston as a professor, teaching, among other things, mathematics and astronomy.

In 1853 Francis W. Capers, who had left to teach in Kentucky, returned to The Citadel and became its superintendent, with the rank of major. The new assistant superintendent was Peter Fayssoux Stevens. That same year, on April 9, Colonel Barnard Bee died at the age of sixty-four in Pendleton and was buried at St. Paul's.

One view of life and conditions at The Citadel at this time was revealed in a series of letters from a cadet, Gilbert Lafayette Strait, who went there in 1854 after one year at the Arsenal. "We are not on an equality in respect to treatment, with yours or any other person's negroes," he said in a letter on February 7, 1854. Strait added in that letter that Charleston was "the nastiest stinkiest triffingist lowest place anywhere to be found" and on parade he said, "Stevens in the most abrupt manner as though he was speaking to a negro ordered him (a cadet officer) to leave the green and consider himself under arrest—a thing never known to be done before." Strait was expelled in July 1854, after problems with another professor. On March 2, 1855, he heard from a cousin, John D. Wylie, who said discipline had become rigid. "We have three or four...under arrest...several fellows have gone home."

The letter also reported, "Old Stevens has gone for five or six days. I think he has gone to marry Mary Capers, major's sister, for it is the 'common talk' in garrison that they are engaged. 'Old Steve' has been looking like a sick kitten for some time & love I presume is his malady." "Old Steve" was twenty-five years old at the time, and it was just a visit to Mary that Wylie wrote about, because it was not until May 1, 1855, that they were married. Her father, the Methodist bishop who had established residence there with his family, conducted services in Anderson. Among those attending was a younger brother, Ellison Capers, who was about to become a Citadel cadet himself.

Henry Kennedy Stevens may have been invited to the wedding, but he wasn't available. On June 21, 1853, a flotilla had left Norfolk, bound for a North Pacific survey and exploration into uncharted waters for the guidance and protection of American whaling vessels, which regularly searched the Arctic waters. To get to the North Pacific from Virginia, it was necessary to go to South Africa, round Cape Horn and proceed north and west again. An assortment of ships in the flotilla caused slow travel, and Acting Lieutenant Stevens was put in command of the *J. Fenimore Cooper*, a schooner that had been used previously as a pilot boat in New York. As each vessel had to sail at its own speed, rendezvous points were established along the way. The first was Simmonstown, False Bay, South Africa, close to Cape Town. Next was Batavia, where Stevens and his schooner crew were detached to survey the Gasper Straits and to take dispatches to Singapore, joining the flotilla again in Hong Kong.

At Hong Kong, Commodore Matthew Perry and his squadron joined the flotilla briefly, fresh from Japan where he had successfully negotiated a treaty of peace and trading rights. Henry Stevens learned he had been promoted to lieutenant, having completed the required fourteen years of service. The flotilla, crippled by the hardships of time and weather, was breaking up. Stevens was given command of the *John Hancock*, which previously had been used mostly in Boston Harbor. He then surveyed the coasts of Japan and the Sea of Okhotsk, while others remaining in the flotilla headed into the Bering Straits and the Aleutians. Finally, the survey over, Stevens made his way back to New York, arriving there in July 1856. He had been gone three years. Shore duty was to follow, as considerable time was needed to prepare the vast number of charts developed during the survey.

By the time Fayssoux and Mary were married in 1855, Clement and Ann Stevens were parents of two sons, Clement and Hamilton. More would follow. Clement had also been promoted several years before that time, becoming cashier of the Planters and Mechanics Bank in 1851. In later years the *Charleston Daily Courier* would comment, "By his business talents he commanded the highest respects of all associated with that institution, and ranked high as a man of financial abilities. By his industry and attention to his own affairs, commencing with out a cent but his salary, he soon secured an independency."

In 1858 Henry Stevens was deeply involved with his survey mapping, and he was deeply in love. Now stationed in Washington, he had met and courted Grace Totten, daughter of Major General Joseph Gilbert Totten, chief engineer of the United States Army. Marriage came on October 28, 1858, in New Haven, Connecticut, where Grace was staying with friends while her parents were out of the country.

In 1849 Hamilton Bee had been elected to the House of Representatives in Texas from his district at Laredo. While still serving in 1854, his wife left him to go back to Mexico with their two children, and Bee—who always was close to the two girls—married Mary Mildred Tarver, from an Alabama family. Bee was elected speaker of the House of Representatives for a two-year term in 1855, and by 1859 he and his family had moved from Laredo and were in Goliad County. The first four of their ten children had been born. During all this time, Captain Barnard E. Bee was serving with the army on the frontier in Minnesota, was on an expedition in Utah and aided in quelling Indian troubles in Dakota and the Northwest. He found time on February 3, 1856, to marry Sophia Hill, daughter of an army man, with ceremonies taking place at Fort Snelling, Minnesota. The first of three children, Ann Fayssoux Bee, was born at Fort Ridgely, Minnesota, on October 29, 1856.

Francis Capers resigned from The Citadel to become president of the Georgia Military Academy. His brother Ellison graduated from The Citadel that year and became an assistant professor of mathematics at the school. On February 24 that year, Ellison married Charlotte Rebecca Palmer, a daughter of John and Catherine Palmer of St. John's at Berkeley. The new superintendent at the South Carolina Military Academy was certainly well known to the Capers family. It was their brother-in-law, Peter Fayssoux Stevens. He was appointed, with the rank of major, on September 8, 1859. The major and his wife, Mary, were by now the parents of two daughters, Mary and Helen. Life was looking rosy for them, for the banker brother and the Capers brother. Navy Lieutenant Henry Stevens probably was sad. Shore duty was over and still almost a newlywed, he was ordered to sea.

INDEPENDENCE DAY

It apparently was destined that Charleston would be the center of attention as the nation awaited the outcome of the threat of Secession. The city had been in the spotlight in the days of the American Revolution, and it was Charlestonians, for the most part, who guided the state into the first half of the nineteenth century. Political observers were almost unanimous in predicting that if war were to come, it would blossom in the Charleston harbor. Certainly the seeds of war were planted there, though many openly observed any seceding would be peaceable, but privately knowing it could not be so simple. The nation's attention was on Charleston from April 23 to May 3, 1860, as the Democratic Party nominating convention met there. Northern delegates dominated the meeting and delegates from Alabama, Arkansas, Florida, Georgia, Louisiana and South Carolina walked out. Remaining delegates, after fifty-seven ballots, were unable to muster a two-thirds majority for a candidate. They adjourned.

On May 9 and 10, the Constitutional Union Party was established in Baltimore and nominated John Bell of Tennessee for the presidency. The party opposed sectionalism and advocated enforcement of the Constitution and the federal laws. The Republican national convention convened in Chicago from May 16 to 20, and while William H. Seward was the favorite candidate, his antislavery position was too radical for many delegates. On the third ballot, Abraham Lincoln of Illinois was nominated. Lincoln had spoken often against slavery, and the South could not digest his views. The Republican Party's platform included antislavery in the territories.

The Democratic Party tried again June 18 to 23 in Baltimore, and more Southern delegates withdrew. Stephen A. Douglas was nominated. The party bolters from Charleston went into Baltimore as the National Democratic Party on June 28 and nominated John C. Breckinridge of Kentucky. On November 6, a decidedly divided voting public elected Lincoln. He received 1,865,593 popular votes and 180 electoral votes. Douglas had 1,382,712 popular votes and 12 electoral votes. Breckinridge received 848,356 popular and 72 electoral votes, and Bell had 592,906 popular and 39 electoral votes. Lincoln carried eighteen free states, Breckinridge had eleven slave states, Bell won three border states and Douglas carried Missouri and three of New Jersey's electoral votes.

With Lincoln's election, South Carolina called a special convention in Columbia but moved to Charleston the following day, due to a smallpox threat. There was a resolution to that effect, as well as one thanking the proper officials regarding the attendance at the inauguration of South Carolina's newest governor—an event declined due to more pressing matters. The day before the Secession Convention convened, the state had elected an Edgefield man with strong Pendleton ties as governor. He was Francis Wilkinson Pickens, grandson of Andrew Pickens, the Revolutionary Patriot, Indian fighter, peacemaker and one of the founders of Pendleton. The new governor's father, also Andrew, had been governor from 1816 to 1818. He was even kin to John C. Calhoun.

Just one day in office, Pickens wrote a letter to President Buchanan claiming that the Federal forts in Charleston Harbor were being prepared to turn their guns on the city. He said the U.S. arsenal had been turned over to South Carolina, and he asked the president to allow him to send a small force to take possession of the uncompleted Fort Sumter. Buchanan was alarmed. The arsenal had not been turned over to South Carolina, and the issue of Fort Sumter was raised for the first time. Pickens was persuaded to withdraw his request.

"On December 20, 1860, South Carolina ceased to be a part of the United States of America," read the headline of the *Daily Courier* on the morning of December 21, as the state seceded from the United States.

It was a holiday for Charlestonians and for most Southerners as word reached them by telegraph. Bells rang, bands played, citizens rejoiced. The day belonged to those citizens of the Holy City of Charleston. Even George Christy's Minstrels, performing on an extended stay in the city, "attended their acceptable services." On Christmas Day, cashier C.H. Stevens signed newspaper advertisements announcing the Planters and Mechanics Bank would pay a dividend of seventy-five cents to stockholders. Lieutenant Henry Kennedy Stevens spent Christmas on the Congo River in Africa. Major Peter Fayssoux Stevens and the Citadel cadets went about their duty, including preparations for what might become a war. It was about this time, too, that Fayssoux apparently started showing an interest in the ministry.

A day after Christmas, a surprise was in store for the nation. At dusk on December 26, the destination unknown by his men until the moment of departure, Major Robert Anderson of the U.S. Army silently moved his troops from Fort Moultrie into Fort Sumter. A shocked Charleston population and an incensed South Carolina government awoke on December 27, discovering the move.

Commissioners were rushed to Washington and state troops went to Castle Pinckney and Fort Moultrie in Charleston Harbor, where the state flag replaced the U.S. flag, just as it did at the Customs House, the post office and the arsenal. The Secession Convention had continued, originally until a Confederacy could be formed, and as the year was ending, resolutions called for the creation of a Southern Confederacy, with representatives to meet in Montgomery, Alabama.

A small item in the December 31, 1860 issue of the *Courier*, all but hidden in other news and almost as if it was a social announcement, stated, "A detachment of the Citadel Cadets under command of MAJOR STEVENS left this city on Sunday for Morris Island."

THE FIRST SHOT

Charleston is on a peninsula between the Cooper and Ashley Rivers. They unite and widen into a harbor lying mostly to the southeast of the city, bounded on the northern line by the mainland and on the south by James Island. Charlestonians will tell you this is where the two rivers come together to form the Atlantic Ocean.

James Island is accessible from the sea on the opposite side, also, through Stono Inlet and River, a deep estuary dividing it from Johns Island on the south. Between Stono Inlet and the entrance of the harbor, a distance of twelve miles, there are two long, low, narrow and sandy Sea Islands—Folly Island and Morris Island—separated from each other by a narrow inlet, and by marshes, about two miles wide, from James Island inside them. Morris Island is nearly four miles long, with its northern end, Cummins Point, being the seaward limit of Charleston Harbor to the south as Sullivan's Island is the limit on the north. These two points determine the entrance to the harbor and are 2,700 yards apart. Sullivan's Island is nearly the same length as Morris Island, having its western extremity farther inside the harbor than Cummins Point and its eastern extremity to Long Island. As on the other side of the harbor, marshes, two miles in width, separate the Sea Islands from the mainland.

Fort Sumter, built upon a shoal and rising out of the water on a man-made rock island, is within the entrance to the harbor, midway between Morris and Sullivan's Islands. Between the fort and the shores of Morris and James Islands there is only shallow water, unfit for navigation. The main channel is very deep between the fort and Sullivan's Island, takes a square turn to the south about a thousand yards east of Fort Sumter, continues straight along the shore of Morris Island, turns sharply to the east, crosses the bar and flows into the ocean eleven miles from the city.

Fort Sumter was named after General Thomas Sumter, who, as "the Gamecock," and with Francis "Swamp Fox" Marion and Andrew "Border Wizard Owl" Pickens, was a partisan officer during the American Revolution. His name often was incorrectly spelled "Sumpter" in later years. The fort was slowly begun in 1829 by the federal government, and it was nearly completed when Major Robert Anderson and his troops occupied it. It is $3\frac{1}{2}$ miles from the East Bay Battery of Charleston. Distances from the fort to the islands range from $\frac{3}{4}$ of a mile to $1\frac{1}{2}$ miles. In January 1861, guns at these points—and the eyes of the nation—were all aimed at Fort Sumter.

Within hours after South Carolina discovered the Federal troops had occupied Fort Sumter, Governor Francis W. Pickens had sent Colonel Johnston Pettigrew and the first regiment of militia rifles, and Colonel W.G. De Saussure and the first regiment of artillery to Fort Moultrie and Castle Pinckney, the last built in 1811 on a shoal near Charleston and having little consequence during the war. Governor Pickens also ordered a battery to be built for two twenty-four-pounders on Morris Island, bearing on Ship Channel, and as 1861 was ushered in, the task was readily being performed by Major P.F. Stevens with a detachment of Citadel cadets, supported by the Vigilant Rifles.

Major Anderson and his Federal troops were virtually without supplies after the South Carolina takeover, having not stocked up before slipping away from Fort Moultrie during the night. South Carolina was in a good position with captured arms and supplies to be ready for war. Reports came from the Northern press that a steamer, the *Star of the West*, had left New York with supplies and some two hundred solders as reinforcements for Fort Sumter. Later articles refuted the move, but on the morning of January 9, 1861, the steamer appeared in the channel headed for the fort.

A Charleston steamer, the *General Clinch*, had left the city on the evening of January 8 with a guard of eighty from the Palmetto Guards and the Irish Volunteers. The assignment was to monitor the harbor and report any Federal ships attempting to enter. At 6:30 a.m. on January 9, signal rockets were fired as a warning. The *Star of the West* entered Ship Channel, adjacent to Morris Island. Major Stevens and his cadets, now joined by Zouave Cadets, the German Riflemen and the Vigilant Rifles, were ready. A shot was fired across the bow of the ship. It was answered by the hoisting of the United States flag. This "act of defiance," reported the *Courier*, "was met with a succession of heavy shots from the fortification."

The vessel continued on its way with increased speed, but one or two shots took effect and advance was slowed. As ineffective fire then followed from Moultrie, the steamer lowered its flag to half-mast and turned to sea with slight damage. Charlestonians, gathered in force along the East Bay Battery, cheered and sought details. Federal troops watched but never raised a gun during the incident.

"Who fired the first shot?" was the question in the minds of many people. The *Courier* credited one person, but official reports confirmed another. Sergeant S.E. Welch of the Zouave Cadets said Cadet W.S. Simkins, on post at the battery, gave the alarm. He said, "The sentinels along the beach took up the call, the long roll was sounded, and the men immediately took their positions: the Citadel cadets at the guns, the Zouave Cadets and German Riflemen just in their rear as infantry support."

Welch said the ship was soon inside the channel and rapidly approaching. The guns were loaded, the lanyards stretched, the men awaiting orders. There seemed to be some hesitation among the higher officers; the commanding officer, evidently impressed with the seriousness of firing on the United States flag, appeared to be in doubt. Major P.F. Stevens, commanding the cadets, turned and gave the command, "Commence firing." The cadet captain passed the order, "Number one fire!" Cadet G.E. Haynesworth, of Sumter, pulled the lanyard and fired the first gun of the war, the shot going across the *Star of the West.* Cadet S.B. Pickens fired the second shot directly at her, and the firing then became general, each gun in turn. The vessel paid no attention to the first shots before slowing down and putting out to sea. Peter Fayssoux Stevens, engineer, mathematician, father, military school leader and a budding minister of the Gospel, had uttered the command for the first act of hostility.

"Major Anderson," wrote Ellison Capers, "acted with great forbearance and judgment, and did not open his batteries. He declared his purpose to be patriotic, and so undoubtedly was." It was Capers's brother-in-law, Fayssoux Stevens, who obviously was being patriotic to South Carolina.

A letter of protest over the incident went to Governor Pickens from Major Anderson. He expressed hope it was not supported by the authority of the state, and if it were he would consider it an act of war and begin firing on all vessels coming within range of his guns.

Pickens said the attempt to bring in supplies and additional troops was in open defiance of the independent state of South Carolina.

He said South Carolina was free of the United States and by sending troops, it was open and hostile disregard for the state. Anderson replied, agreeing to send the matter to the government in Washington, and declared a truce until he received his orders. The time was used by both sides to make preparations for the war certain to come. There obviously was reluctance, North and South, because incidents had already occurred that could have gone into history as the starting point. The North and some Southern states at the time could say South Carolina's act of Secession was the signal. South Carolina could say it was Major Anderson's covert move into Fort Sumter that was the war signal. The North could reply that it was the immediate seizure of Federal property by South Carolina that was the initial action. Even some Southerners felt the "Palmetto Republic" had acted too hastily.

Major Stevens and his Citadel cadets were the toast of the town. Mere teenagers, most of them never even away from home before enrolling at the military academy, were thrown into a limelight, which would shine brighter before it faded and burned out. On January 15, 1861, the *Charleston Mercury* printed portions of an article from the *New York Evening Post*, written by a reporter who had sailed with the steamer to Charleston and had given full reports along the way. The article said the military men on board complimented South Carolina on its shooting, and "one of the officers hazarded a joke soon after we left Charleston harbor. 'The people of South Carolina,' he remarked, 'pride themselves upon their hospitality, but it exceeded my expectation—they gave us several <u>balls</u> before we landed!'"

Fayssoux Stevens resigned as superintendent of the South Carolina Military Academy. He had completed two years of training as a minister, and he turned his full attention to Trinity Church at Black Oak—for a while. Later, Clement Hoffman Stevens had recovered from his wounds and with no military knowledge formed and began training the Sixteenth Regiment, South Carolina Militia—for a while. It's hard to keep a good man down.

Henry Kennedy Stevens arrived on the USS *Portsmouth* at Portsmouth, New Hampshire, on September 24, 1861. He was immediately arrested and committed to Fort Lafayette in New York harbor, and by order of President Lincoln his name was stricken from the rolls of the U.S. Navy on September 30, 1861. What had been the advice of his father-in-law, General Totten, and his kinsman Commodore Shubrick, during those agonizing times as Hal groped for a decision? Though correspondence or official papers have never been found except for his June resignation from London, the official records of prisoners of war state he resigned on March 25, 1861. It was a resignation, for certain, but the official rolls of the U.S. Navy, showing various stations and commands written in small letters, has bold and underlined words by Hal's name reading "September 30, 1861. Dismissed." Stevens found some eighty other prisoners at Fort Lafayette when he arrived, many of them political prisoners, some from the U.S. Navy and a few from the U.S. Army. Among the "prisoners of state" was S. Teackle Wallis, one of the noted Maryland orators and writers of the day. His law partner was John H. Thomas, whose sister-in-law was Mrs. Mary Fayssoux (John Chew) Leiper.

Grace Totten Stevens had returned from Maderia and was able to visit Hal in prison. However, fifty-three of the prisoners, along with fourteen imprisoned after a petition to free them, were transferred to Fort Warren in Boston Harbor. Among them were Wallis and Stevens, and bargaining for prisoner exchanges began. Stevens and three others were transferred from Fort Warren to the frigate USS *Congress*, off Newport News, Virginia, as negotiations to free them began. Grace Totten Stevens was in Virginia during all this, having come under a flag of truce from New York to seek her husband's release without pledge or parole, to be exchanged for Lieutenant Kautz, U.S. Navy.

After eight weeks in prison, and after two years abroad before then, Hal Stevens stepped ashore on his native soil. There was Grace, and except for the brief visit with her at Fort Lafayette, they had not been together since he left her in Maderia in the summer of 1859. Grace had made her decision—her place was with her husband, no matter where he might be—but she expressed love for her native North. While she was saddened at being cut off from her family, she knew she had a new one in the South.

Hal Stevens, briefly a civilian now, made plans for Grace and him to go first to Richmond, then to Charleston and finally to Spartanburg, where his mother, Sarah (of Pendleton), was visiting her daughters. He also telegraphed South Carolina Governor Francis W. Pickens, offering his services to the state, and unless there were other uses for him, he proposed to enter the navy.

On November 7, 1861, a Union squadron of seventy-four vessels and twelve thousand troops under Flag Officer Samuel F. DuPont and General Thomas W. Sherman occupied Port Royal Sound, South Carolina. The war was coming back to the Palmetto Republic.

News of Secession had reached the USS *Portsmouth* in March 1861, but it was well after the fall of Fort Sumter before Lieutenant Henry Kennedy Stevens's letter to his father-in-law would reach him, and it would be June before his decision regarding the U.S. Navy was official. While the navy officer's letter was en route to General Joseph Gilbert Totten, Virginia, Arkansas and North Carolina seceded from the Union, and in Tennessee the western and central portions of the state favored the move. There was enough Union sentiment in eastern Tennessee to allow U.S. Senator Andrew Johnson to remain in Washington. The Confederate Congress declared that a state of war existed with the United States, Abraham Lincoln called for more troops; the Confederates moved the capital from Montgomery to Richmond, Virginia; and Union troops crossed the Potomac River and occupied Alexandria, Virginia.

Lincoln ordered a naval blockade of Charleston, and South Carolina troops geared up to defend the city. Superintendent Peter Fayssoux turned his attention back to the South Carolina Military Academy and, pursuing a religious call that had developed some months earlier, also became pastor-in-training of Trinity, Black Oak, Protestant Episcopal Church near Charleston. Here he was, married into a prominent family, but going into the pulpit of an Episcopal church like one he had grown up attending in Pendleton, except the black worshippers at Black Oak were far larger in number.

Up Against a Stone Wall

Confederate President Jefferson Davis, impressed with Barnard E. Bee because of his military knowledge in the West before the war, promoted him to brigadier general and placed him in command of the Third Brigade of the Army of the Shenandoah under Brigadier General Joseph R. Johnston. Bee's brigade consisted of the Fourth Alabama, Second and Eleventh Mississippi and First Tennessee infantries, along with Imboden's Battery. As Bee headed to Virginia to assume his command, he took a volunteer aide-de-camp with him: his banker brother-in-law, Clement Hoffman Stevens.

Henry Kennedy Stevens's letter, written at sea on March 26, 1861, likely did not reach General Totten until May, and it included a copy of his resignation from the navy. He advised he was writing Grace to go home "and shall desire my brother to place two hundred dollars in your hands for her use," unless it had already been done. In a postscript, Stevens said he had suggested in his letter to Shubrick that an immediate and unconditional resignation might be in order. "I say the same to you Sir: for there is no knowing what may be the state of things when this reaches you." What was the agony of Stevens and all others aboard the ship, Northern and Southern alike? What, too, were General Totten and Commodore Shubrick to do?

Totten, born and bred in the North, had a daughter who may have moved to the South, cut off from him. Shubrick, a native Charlestonian, had spent most of his life in the U.S. Navy and had seen and known little of the South for many years. The resignation Stevens mentioned as being enclosed never became a part of the records. The "state of things" were certainly known by June, and whether it was altered advice or on his own, Stevens, in the harbor of London, wrote Navy Secretary Gideon Wells on June 12, 1861: "Sir, With much regret, I find myself under the necessity of leaving the Service. I therefore tender this resignation of my commission as a Lieutenant in the Navy of the United States."

Colonel Robert E. Lee had resigned his commission in the United States Army in the spring of 1861 and was placed in command of Confederate troops in Virginia. That state had not been as certain on Secession, and while Virginia did secede, a group of delegates from the western part gathered in Wheeling to defend the Union. General George McClellan moved into what later would be West Virginia and defeated a small Confederate force at Philippi in June 1861. Later in the month, Union troops under General Nathaniel Lyon took control of the lower Missouri River. Still later, McClellan's forces were declared the winners in several skirmishes in western Virginia. Confederate troops took a few other small campaigns along the Potomac River.

Generally, Confederate battles were designated by whatever town was nearby. Union listings normally referred to a body of water in the vicinity. In July 1861, troops began centering attention on a small town in Virginia selected by the Confederates as a key point to stop advances to Richmond—the goal of the Union army. The Southern forces had the high ground at the town of Manassas Junction. Union troops set up defense at a nearby river named Bull Run. (I had a lady who once told me she had applied for membership in the United Daughters of the Confederacy and never heard from them. She couldn't understand it because she said her ancestor fought at Bull Run. Figure that one out.)

Response was swift in both the North and South after Fort Sumter. By mid-July, as battle loomed at Manassas, Union forces under Brigadier General Irvin McDowell numbered 35,000. Southern forces included the Army of the Shenandoah under General Joseph E. Johnston and the Army of the Potomac under General P.G.T. Beauregard—a total Confederate force of 18,053.

As the first major battle of the war, Manassas—or Bull Run—is well documented, and has been described in detail many times. One of the major forces in that campaign was Barnard Elliott Bee. One unpublished account of some of the activity comes from Clement Stevens, in a letter to his brother-in-law, Hamilton Bee. Clement said

General Joseph Johnston's army was at Winchester, Virginia, about 9,000 strong, with Bee a part of it with four regiments in a brigade. Reinforcements brought the Confederate force up to 15,000. Union General Robert Patterson had 25,000 men at Martinsburg, and Stevens wrote: "Patterson advanced and threatened us several times, but finally turned off…to Charlestown, the same day we rec orders to make a forced march to Manassas, and join Beauregard."

Bee arrived by train on Saturday, July 20, with two regiments and his staff. Their horses, coming by land, had not arrived. The unit was forced to an advance position where a Union assault was expected, and when it did not materialize, the troops

> *lay that day and night in the woods. It was 6 a.m. on July 21 when Stevens said Bee received orders to take his and Francis Bartow's brigade and move to the left. Our horses arrived at that opportune moment…We marched about seven miles to find that the enemy had already driven Shank Evans from Stone Bridge and were outflanking us to the left. [Bee] did not wait for orders, but re-established lines further left, placing Imboden's Battery directly opposite William T. Sherman's battery. We were 300 yards from the enemy and continued to advance until the 4th Alabama Regt, which I carried into position, was within 100 yards of the advance. He [Bee] passed to other positions while I was finding my presence useful with the 4th Ala and remained with them and rallied them several times.*

Six months earlier Clement Stevens was quietly at work in a Charleston bank, and now was in the midst, as a civilian, of a major battle. Union regular army forces were opposite him "and the balls rained on us in all directions. The air was filled with their rifle muskets and artillery. It was a perfect storm." Stevens said his men could lie down while loading, but he and the field officers were mounted and exposed. "I was shot a Minnie ball entering about 4 inches above the hip joint on the right side ranging around the back bone and coming out opposite where it started." Riding off to get aid, and bleeding freely, Stevens said he was under heavy fire going up a hill and "half way up a 9 lb shot tore up the earth under my horses feet. I sprang from my saddle picked up the ball and continued my course." Here was an exposed, wounded man, stopping for a souvenir.

The wound happened about 2:00 p.m. on July 21, and Stevens was not allowed to go back into battle. "Poor B was very much distressed thinking I had been killed," he wrote. As the battle went on, Bee had his own hands full, however. As the Union attack strengthened, General Beauregard described the activity, saying he and General Johnston arrived just as Bee's troops, after giving way, were fleeing in disorder behind the height in rear of Stone Bridge.

They had come around between the base of the hill and the Stone Bridge into a shallow ravine, which ran up to a point on the crest where Jackson had already formed his brigade along the edge of the woods. Jackson was Thomas Jonathan Jackson of Virginia. Beauregard said futile attempts were made to reform lines. Reports said, "Voices mingling with the noise of the shells were hurtling through the trees overhead, and all word of command drowned in the confusion and uproar. It was at this moment that General Bee used the famous expression, 'Look at Jackson's brigade. It stands like a stone wall!'—a name that passed from the brigade to its immortal commander."

Just as Manassas–Bull Run is fought today by reenactment groups and by armchair generals, that statement continues to be one of issue. Just what did Bee say, and in what vein did he say it? Colonel J.B.E. Sloan of Pendleton, in his narrative of the Fourth Regiment of South Carolina Volunteers, said, "Gen. Bee and Col. Sloan, riding forward, exhorting the men into line, Gen. Bee shouted 'See Jackson's men standing like a stonewall.' 'Jackson,' said a friend, 'with characteristic modesty, always insisted that Bee had referred to his brigade and not to himself personally.'" (Another battle, which continued long after the war—in print—was between Generals Beauregard and Johnston, along with Jefferson Davis, over who was in charge of what and who did this or that, or who didn't.)

The monument to Bee at Manassas, which was placed by the Mary Taliaferro Thompson Southern Memorial Association, bears this quotation: "Form, form. There stands Jackson like a stone wall. Rally around the Virginians."

There are modern-day references to the incident, which question whether the war cry was one to spur on the troops, or to observe that Jackson was doing nothing. Some have even commented that Bee's brother-in-law said it was an adverse statement, but family members have found no reference to the incident in Stevens's papers. However, he wasn't at the scene, having been wounded and away from action. Whatever, and remember General Beauregard said there were bursting shells, yelling and confusion, the Stone Bridge was the deciding factor for the South that day. It resulted in a rout of the Union troops all the way back to Washington. Some Northern observers, however, say it was a necessary retreat but hampered by Washington citizens who had brought picnic lunches and watched the battle, then clogged the road trying to flee.

Why, with all the variations, did Barnard E. Bee not ever make it clear? In the battle that ensued, Bee was struck down, mortally wounded. That was the primary reason Clement Stevens was writing Hamilton Bee in Texas on July 28, as he was recuperating in Charleston. He had begun the letter by saying:

> *Long before this reaches you the Telegraph will have told of the events of Sunday the 21 July. It will have told you we have been called to pay our tribute of blood to this glorious cause in which we are engaged; that we have sacrificed our brightest hopes upon the altars of our liberty. Our Barnard, the brother of our hopes and our hearts, the loved one of our family circle, the General of our Countries armies, lies in a soldiers grave. He fell on the field of his fame and leaves no blot on his character. Stern hearted warriors wept bitter tears, as he passed from the field of glory.*

Colonel J.B.E. Sloan wrote, after the cry by Bee, that Bee's men and the five companies of the Fourth South Carolina Regiment and others surged into line and fought back and forth across the Warrenton Turnpike until the end of the battle, during which the

Fourth Regiment had been under nearly continuous fire for seven hours. It was during one of these advances that the gallant Bee fell wounded while leading a charge.

Accounts at the time say when he fell Bee was grasping the sword the State of South Carolina had presented to him for his valor in the Mexican War. Doctor Rodger Stroup, now the state archivist and once chief curator of the South Carolina State Museum where the sword is displayed, says it is not true. The mint condition of the sword shows no wear, and even one day on horseback would have revealed wear. Besides, it was a ceremonial sword only and had no sharpened blade.

Bee had fallen a few yards back of the Henry house, occupied by a woman who had refused to leave her home and who was killed during the battle. It was being used as Confederate headquarters, and on learning he was there, Stevens wrote Hamilton that he dressed, and with the aid of two soldiers, walked two hundred yards to the room where Bee lay. "When I took his hand he said, 'Well old fellow, I thought they had got you.' My wound had commenced to bleed freely which with the exertion of walking and perhaps the excitement overcame me and for the first time in my life I fainted."

Bee's wound in the groin and hip occurred about 3:15 p.m. on July 21. He died at 11:20 a.m. the following day. Confederate President Davis had come from Richmond to view the Manassas situation, and wrote later in his book: "When riding to the front I met an ambulance bearing Gen. Bee from the field where he had been mortally wounded after his patriotism had been illustrated by conspicuous exhibitions of skill, daring and fortitude.

"When he fell mortally wounded his thoughts were of that of home, for which he called out, 'Where are the Pendleton boys? Let them take me off the field', and some of them did."

Colonel Sloan wrote: "Gen. Bee fell mortally wounded near the Henry house and was taken from the field after the battle by Capt. Kilpatrick and Privates Russell, Dickson, Harris and Seaborn, all of the Fourth Regiment. Arriving at the Manassas road Gen. Bee being greatly exhausted was laid alongside the road. Cheering down the road revealed President Davis and party approaching. The President dismounted and with tearful eyes approached Gen. Bee and expressed the greatest solicitude and earnestly prayed that his life might be spared to his family and his country."

Generals Beauregard and Johnston agreed on one thing. Both had high praise for Bee and most other observers said the actions of Bee and Francis Bartow were the deciding factors in the battle. Stevens told Hamilton Bee "Genl Beauregard sends word that…if it had not been for him he would not say what the day might have been!"

The bodies of Bee, Bartow (who had been killed almost at the same moment as Bee) and Lieutenant Colonel B.J. Johnson lay in state in Richmond and then went by train to Charleston, arriving July 27. Bartow's body was later removed to Savannah, Georgia, where he had been mayor. Newspaper accounts of the day said when the train arrived, with many people waiting, "Clement Stevens was aboard…accompanied by his brother, Major P.F. Stevens of the Citadel Academy. Mr. Stevens…was reclining on a litter, and had the appearance of having suffered severely. With help, he was placed in a carriage and taken to his home. The bodies were escorted to the city hall, which had been draped in mourning. Bells tolled, flags flew at half-staff, and stores closed and…between 4,000 and 5,000 people viewed the bodies laid out in state."

The funeral services almost paralleled the one for John C. Calhoun. These were the first Southern officers to die, and ceremony would never be so massive again, as almost daily trains would later be bringing bodies home.

Henry Kennedy Stevens was at sea, still not knowing what reaction he would receive when he set foot on land in a divided nation. Fayssoux Stevens was about to leave The Citadel. Clement, in his letter to Hamilton, said, "Battles are over unless they come here to attack us…I have too many dependent on me now to risk my life unless compelled to."

Compelling reasons were not far away.

The summer of 1861 saw Charleston and all of coastal South Carolina setting up defenses against expected Union attack. On August 21, Brigadier General R.S. Ripley, a native of Ohio, was assigned to the command of the Department of South Carolina and its coastal defenses. Ripley had distinguished himself in the United States Army, particularly during the Mexican War. He married into the Middleton family of Charleston and left the army in 1859 to reside there. On the fall of Fort Sumter, he donned a Confederate uniform.

Enterprising Clement Stevens, recovering from wounds and establishing a militia company, had also gone into business. He and St. Julien Ravenel established the Colleton Lime Works and Henry W. Ravenel, visiting there on October 30, 1861, said they "have been doing a profitable business since the blockade. Henry Ravenel said 'Pa and I rode to Stone Landing…to see the place and operations of barrel making and lime burning…They are turning out 100 barrels per day and sell it readily at $2.00 per bar.'" How long the business operated is not known, but the price was fair and could not have been considered profiteering.

The Reverend Peter Fayssoux Stevens, for the time being, continued his church work, but it soon would be interrupted. Ellison Capers remained at The Citadel, and that too would change soon. Hamilton P. Bee remained on duty in Texas.

When word came to Governor Francis W. Pickens that a fleet and troops were headed for Port Royal, he urged additional Confederate forces be sent to the state. Available troops were already active elsewhere. Battles were taking place in Virginia, North Carolina, Tennessee, Missouri and the West—throughout the embattled nations. The superior force of the Union fleet and armed troops were too much for Port Royal at Hilton Head. Despite two Confederate forts there, heavy firepower caused a retreat to Beaufort. On November 7, the Union took Port Royal, establishing a secure base for its navy, with safe and comfortable camping grounds on the numerous islands for the Union army under General T.W. Sherman.

Ellison Capers observed after the war

> *The effect of this Union victory was to give the fleet and army of the United States a permanent and abundant base of operations against*

the whole coast of South Carolina, and against either Charleston or Savannah, as the Federal authorities might elect…The occupation caused immediate abandonment of the whole sea-island country around Beaufort. The planters hastened away, leaving their estates to pillage and ruin. Thousands of slaves fell into the hands of the Union forces. General Sherman advised that not a single white inhabitant remained on the islands of Hilton Head, St. Helena, Ladies and Port Royal.

On November 8, the day after the fall of Port Royal, the Confederate government placed the Virginian General Robert E. Lee in command of the departments of South Carolina and Georgia. He immediately asked General Ripley for an assessment of the situation, and it resulted in withdrawing all Confederate forces from the islands and strengthening the mainland, particularly around Charleston.

Peter Fayssoux Stevens had answered the call to be a minister, and he was beginning well with his church, but as war was imminent in his beloved South Carolina, he had a stronger call to help defend it. In November 1861, he offered his services to Governor Pickens to raise a legion consisting of infantry, artillery and cavalry. He was changing clerical robes for a uniform again. Governor Pickens commissioned the Holcombe Legion, with P.F. Stevens as its commander, on November 21, 1861. The origin of naming the legion was confirmed in later years, it being in honor of Lucy Holcombe Pickens, wife of the governor.

The Citadel did not close during the war, although the war was almost at its door. Union forces explored the islands near Charleston during the winter, and set up a base on Edisto Island. Confederate forces were dispatched to hold them off, the island being but twenty-five miles from Charleston. Family reunions can be joyous times. Such was the case with the Stevens brothers. As 1861 was coming to an end with all in Charleston, it was the first time in nearly four years they had been at one place at the same time. Brief visits to Pendleton and Spartanburg occupied some of the time, but while it was a happy time for the family, there was also the watchful eye of what was going to become of them, and of South Carolina and the Confederacy.

A military order on January 21, 1862, proved to be a unique way for a continued reunion:

COL. P.F. STEVENS,
Commanding Holcombe Legion

SPECIAL ORDERS NO. 10

HEADQUARTERS SECOND MILITARY DIST. S.C.
Charleston, January 21, 1862

I. An expedition to act against the enemy in North Edisto will proceed to Seabrook's Island without delay.
Captain Ives, engineer, C.S. Army, will have charge of the attack, being informed of the desires of the brigadier general commanding, and his directions will be obeyed accordingly.
Captain Alfred Rhett, S.C. Artillery, will have charge of the firing party, and will receive instructions to open fire from Captain Ives. Col. Clement H. Stevens, volunteer aide-de-camp, will detail from the unattended troops in camp near the junction of Wappoo and Stono Rivers such infantry force as is requisite for support. II. Lieut. H.K. Stevens, C.S. Navy, is detailed as ordnance officer, and will report and communicate with Captains Ives and Rhett.
By order of Brigadier General Ripley:
LEO D. WALKER Assistant Adjutant-General

Clem, Hal and Fayssoux truly were a band of brothers.

The earliest action was with slaves. Brigadier General Nathan G. Evans, commanding the Third Military District, reported January 25 that Colonel P.F. Stevens had succeeded in capturing about fifty black people on Edisto Island. In his report, Colonel Stevens indicated there were about eighty blacks. Many he had captured were identified by name and by whom they were owned. Due to a Union gunboat firing in the distance, many others already captured managed to escape. He reported, "I regret to state that at the Legare and Seabrook places 3 negroes were either shot or drowned and a fourth wounded; 2 women and 1 man ran into the water, and refusing or failing to come out, were fired upon and disappeared beneath the water."

He advised he seized nine mules, ten horses, five colts, eight carts, one two-horse wagon, two carriages and one buggy. The animals and carts he considered for public service, but the colts were bought by some of the men. Some three hundred to four hundred bushels of corn were burned, along with some cotton.

SPECIAL ORDER NO. 10 did not result in much other activity, except for firing on Union gunboats trying to approach Edisto. After a short while, both Clement and Henry would be departing for other duty, but at least they were all together for a while.

Clem, along with Ellison Capers, had in December 1861 begun raising a new regiment for twelve months of Confederate service. By January 1862, six companies were in camp being instructed. The two men circulated handbills, which stated:

> *The undersigned are engaged in raising*
> *a regiment for the*
> DEFENCE OF THE STATE!
> *A camp has been established near*
> *Charleston, where Companies joining us*
> *will be equipped and furnished with a*
> COMPLETE UNIFORM,
> *including shoes and overcoats. We earn-*
> *estly invite our fellow-citizens to join us*
> *in our effort to*
> DEFEND OUR HOMES AND OUR LIBERTIES!
> *And to drive out enemies from the soil*
> *they have invaded.*

Clem Stevens, still with no formal military training, was learning as he went, happily volunteering for duty on Edisto Island while his planned regiment was being formed.

Union land forces managed to set up a garrison on Edisto Island in February, coming from Port Royal. Early in March, General Robert E. Lee was called to Richmond and placed in command of the armies of the Confederacy, and General John Clifford Pemberton was promoted to major general and placed in command of South Carolina and Georgia. Major General David Hunter had replaced General Sherman as commander of the Union forces, and reported about seventeen thousand troops scattered along the South Carolina coast. Some fourteen hundred of them were on Edisto, advanced to the northern part of the island, with a strong guard on the Little Edisto.

General N.G. Evans sought to capture the guard on Little Edisto in order to block Union troops from coming onto the mainland. The assignment went to Colonel P.F. Stevens and the Holcombe Legion. It was an assignment carried out well. Units numbering in excess of four hundred men went onto the island. Unlike the Beaufort area, where planters had abandoned their homes, people like planters Edward and Henry Seabrook were with the Holcombe Legion as guides, showing shortcuts and little-known paths and river crossings. In predawn darkness and fog on the morning of March 29, 1862, the Holcombe Legion succeeded. Skirmishes with the Union forces resulted in twenty-one persons dead, wounded or captured. Control of the Little Edisto was now in the hands of the Confederates. In his official report, General Evans said in closing, "I would call attention of the general commanding to the dauntless conduct of Major [F.G.] Palmer [Holcombe Legion] and his command. Crossing the bridge over the Little Edisto River, in obedience to his instructions he burned the bridge to his rear and vigorously charged the enemy, determined to conquer or die for the defense of his country."

Palmer, his men and his prisoners had to come back to the mainland with repeated trips in one small boat, which could only hold five people at one time. General Evans also reported, "To Col. P.F. Stevens I am greatly indebted for the skill and gallantry with which he conducted the expedition, to which is due its entire success." Clement Stevens, along with Capers, was training six companies they had raised when the state military council advised no more twelve-month enlistments would be allowed. Agreement was reached to create a regiment if six more companies were formed, all to serve for the duration of the war. Volunteers came freely, just as they did in many parts of the South and a draft had not been necessary.

On April 1, 1862, the Twenty-Fourth Regiment, South Carolina Volunteers, was mustered into service with Colonel C.H. Stevens as commander, supported by Lieutenant Colonel Ellison Capers and Major A.J. Hammond. Clem, like so many others during the war, finally turned his back on business and profession to fight for the Cause. He had tasted war at Manassas, and despite his earlier comments that he was through with the military, he was going to war.

All three brothers were still in Charleston, as were their wives, and perhaps there was some celebration on the mustering of the new regiment. There were also some goodbyes. Early in April, Henry Kennedy Stevens received orders to report to Memphis, Tennessee, for naval duty.

DELIVERED FROM THE VIOLENT MAN

By the end of May 1862, General Stonewall Jackson and his command had gained control of most of the Shenandoah Valley and were threatening Washington, just fifty miles away. General Robert E. Lee had assumed command of the Confederate forces. On July 17, orders came for Brigadier General N.G. Evans to proceed at once toward Richmond with eight batteries, along with Fayssoux Stevens's Holcombe Legion. Troops in South Carolina were being depleted, but the Twenty-fourth Regiment remained.

In August, the Holcombe Legion became involved in battles along the Rappahannock River, and later in the month Evans was ordered to take command of three brigades and he placed Stevens in charge of his own brigade at Manassas Junction with the rank of acting brigadier general. Considerable fighting erupted there and Stevens became separated from his unit, mingling with other troops. When it was all over and everyone was back in the units where they belonged, the Holcombe Legion counted 14 officers and 93 enlisted men killed and 48 officers and 463 enlisted men wounded. Five days earlier Union forces were five miles from Richmond and the Confederates were five miles from Washington, but General Lee chose to change course and help protect Maryland in a show of support.

On September 14, Evans was ordered to march in the direction of Sharpsburg, Maryland, and the forces arrived there a day later. The troops stopped at the Antietam River, which would become one of the deadliest battles in the entire war. Fayssoux Stevens was injured, but survived; many others did not. It still was Sharpsburg in the South, but is mostly known as the Battle of Antietam. The National Cemetery established there in 1862 marks the graves of 4,833 soldiers. The total number of casualties numbered 26,193, counting dead, wounded and missing. A week later, Stevens submitted his resignation.

Here was a man who trained cadets at The Citadel on how to fight in battle. He also taught courses in religion and he often was in prayer, in camp and on the bloody battlefield. Perhaps it was all of the things he had witnessed and taken part in during the previous months, or it was his unwavering faith in his religion, and memories of peaceful times as a child in Pendleton, or the joy of bringing a soul into his church at Black Oak. Perhaps he remembered and read again from II Samuel 23:49–50: "And that bringeth me forth from thine enemies: thou also hast lifted me up on high above them that rose up against me: thou has delivered me from the violent man. Therefore I will give thanks to thee O Lord, among the heathen, and I will sing praises unto thy name."

(When first writing this, I felt there needed to be something scriptural. I randomly opened my Bible to search for a proper quote, and it opened to the page identified here. Twilight zone?)

HEARTACHES AWAY FROM WAR

Barely a year after he left to form the Holcombe Legion, Fayssoux Stevens was back in the fall of 1862 as pastor at Trinity, Black Oak, Episcopal Church. He returned home to find his brother Clement still commanding troops on east James Island. Lieutenant Colonel Ellison Capers had temporary command of the Twenty-fourth

Regiment. About the same time Hal Stevens received a commission from the secretary of the navy promoting him to first lieutenant in the Confederate States navy.

Hal and the others who had escaped after the demise of the *Arkansas* were at Yazoo City to help in defending the Yazoo River. The *Star of the West*, now in Confederate hands, was being repaired and covered with iron. Union forces were approaching so the Confederates scuttled and sunk the ship to keep it from falling into Union hands. One Stevens had shot at it as a prelude to the war and it was destroyed by another brother, twenty months later and seven hundred miles away.

At home, there were heartaches away from war, as three-year-old Barnard Bee, namesake for his father and grandfather, died. Less than two months later Sophia Bee, not yet two years old, joined other family members in death and ended the General Barnard E. Bee family line.

The deaths certainly brought sadness to Clement Stevens and other family members, who were refugees in Pendleton to be away from the powder keg situation in Charleston. But for the dashing colonel the worst was yet to come. On November 8, 1862, his beloved wife of fourteen years, Ann Fayssoux Bee Stevens, died in Pendleton of the same yellow fever attributed to the children's deaths. She was forty-four years old.

Before the agony could diminish, Clement saw his four-year-old son, Lionel Kennedy Stevens, die in Pendleton on November 10, just a few months short of his seventh birthday. In Charleston, Mary Fayssoux Stevens, called Maynie and daughter of the Reverend and Mrs. Peter Fayssoux Stevens, died and was buried in Magnolia Cemetery there. Back in Pendleton, Clement's second son, Hamilton Bee Stevens, age nine, was laid to rest at St. Paul's alongside his mother and other family members. Only Clement Bee Stevens remained.

In August 1862, skirmishes continued in South Carolina, as well as in Virginia, Mississippi, Kentucky and Arkansas. In North Carolina, assistance was deemed needed in the Wilmington area, and among those sent there were Colonel Clem Stevens and the brigade he was temporarily commanding. The expected attack never came, and the Confederate brigade was returned to South Carolina. It resulted in

Clem regaining his Twenty-fourth Regiment command, and it stayed until the end of the year with no activity, as the Union troops had decided to spend the winter in New Bern and not attack elsewhere. Perhaps it was pleasing to him that 1862 was ending after all the tribulations the family had faced in the previous months. In January 1863 there would be more anguish.

WHEN COTTON WASN'T KING

Hal Stevens had received orders instructing him to proceed to the Bayou Teche and examine the steamer *J.A. Cotton*, which he found to be in excellent shape and well equipped with ordnance. He was an observer on board on the morning of January 14, 1863, as it made its way down the Bayou Teche in search of a Union force reported to be advancing both by land and water some twelve miles from Franklin, Louisiana. As the *Cotton* moved along the Teche, heavy firing from Union forces and approaching gunboats caused the Confederate gunners and pilots to abandon their posts and seek cover.

Heavy fire erupted from the shore and Confederate land troops were trying to get in position when Union gunfire increased, and while most of the *Cotton*'s crew were protected behind iron rails, the officers had no such protection. The captain was shot in both arms, five were killed and eight others wounded. The Seminole Indians had not bothered Henry Kennedy Stevens when he was an infant, and he had gone through some twenty years traveling the world at sea with barely a scratch. He died from a bullet wound on the *Cotton* and was just an observer. He was thirty-eight years old.

Grace Totten Stevens, who had traveled with her husband, was in Louisiana and had to make the sad, lonely trip back to Pendleton. Hal was buried near Franklin, Louisiana. Clement was still in North Carolina, as yet unknowing of Hal's death. In the midst of a war at Charleston's doorstep Fayssoux Stevens as secretary-treasurer of the Association of Citadel Men took out a newspaper notice to say a number of members were arrears in dues and should submit the money for the work of the association. Recent graduates were invited to join for five dollars. He gave Black Oak as his mailing address.

In March, a Union naval fleet had moved up the Mississippi River past the Confederate-held Port Hudson, and General U.S. Grant's troops were nearing Vicksburg. South Carolina was ordered to send what available units there might be to Mississippi. It included the Twenty-fourth with Ellison Capers in command. While Clem had returned from North Carolina, he was staying behind to gather supplies to be taken to the unit. There are strong indications he left the supply train along the way to go to Pendleton and visit his mother and son. While Capers said he commanded the troops the entire time in the Vicksburg area, official records show Clem was commanding the entire time. Official records even show he ordered stationery and quills and he signed as colonel, Twenty-fourth Regiment. In a battle on May 14 near Jackson, Mississippi, the Twenty-fourth was trying to set up a defense and, badly outnumbered, had to retreat into Jackson. Ellison Capers was injured and 105 members of the Twenty-Fourth were killed, wounded or captured.

A General Consensus

Charleston's forces had been depleted with the removal of troops to Tennessee and Mississippi and others were in Virginia with Robert E. Lee. In the famed, or infamous if you like, three-day battle at Gettysburg, the North prevailed. As Lee was retreating, U.S. Grant was taking Vicksburg. In July, a siege was renewed in Charleston and by August Fort Sumter was in rubble, its guns replaced by infantry. Still it held out. Mississippi was mainly under Union control and Southern forces, including Clem Stevens's Twenty-fourth Regiment, were moved toward Tennessee, waiting in Rome, Georgia, in reserve.

In the middle of August, Northern troops were in Chattanooga and the Confederates moved out, not in retreat but to wait for reinforcements, which were on the way. The Southern stand was made in northern Georgia, a few miles south of Chattanooga on Chickamauga Creek. In September, forces were ready on both sides of the waterway. Losses were heavy as battles began on September 19, and by September 20 the Twenty-fourth had arrived. Stevens had two horses shot out from under him and was wounded himself. Capers had a horse disabled when it was shot in the thigh.

The South actually prevailed and the troops were quartered for the winter at nearby Dalton, Georgia. It was there on January 24, 1864, that C.H. Stevens was promoted to brigadier general. It was a good choice in the minds of all, and even Confederate President Jefferson Davis had been campaigning for the promotion. Stevens's own men were highly in favor of him and biographies often mentioned, without detail, that he had invented a portable oven so his troops could have fresh bread.

Ellison Capers was promoted to colonel and stayed with the Twenty-fourth. Stevens's new brigade was composed mainly of Georgia regiments, and while he wasn't pleased with them, little was done to change. He reported "too many of them thought they were going to be posted to picket duty in Florida." Stevens was getting the trappings of a general, however, as he paid $228 to the Confederate ordnance store in Macon, Georgia, for items that included an officer's saddle, an officer's bridle and an officer's saddlebag.

Elsewhere, Hamilton Bee, who had been promoted to brigadier general, had been attending to administrative duties and finally was called into action. Trying to protect Texas, his troops stopped a Union attempt to cross the Red River from Shreveport, Louisiana, even though General William T. Sherman had supplied ten thousand men. Texas remained in Confederate hands and Bee remained in the army until the end of the war.

In Chattanooga, General William T. Sherman succeeded U.S. Grant and was ordered to move out. The target was Atlanta, a growing city but still not the capital of the state of Georgia. Early in May, Sherman began his advance. It had no direct connection to the war, but on May 8 in Pendleton—the peaceful town never touched by the guns of war—Sarah Fayssoux Stevens, widow and mother, died at the age of sixty-nine. The brave woman never knew where her husband was buried in Florida. Her son Henry lay buried in Louisiana; son Fayssoux

Stevens ministered in Charleston, his back turned to the war; and her eldest, Clement, was about to step into battle again.

As Sherman advanced the Southerners moved back to Peachtree Creek on the outskirts of Atlanta. The hope to keep the Union forces from crossing was failing and in a heated battle. While Clem was cheering on his men, his horse fell dead on top of him, and his soldiers came to lift him up. He had scarcely risen to his feet when a Minnie ball struck him from behind the right ear, penetrating his brain.

General Stevens was removed to a hospital in Macon, Georgia, by train, away from the battle. On July 25, 1864, his death was entered into the hospital records. He was reported buried at Magnolia Cemetery in Charleston two days later. Not long afterward both his remains and those of Barnard E. Bee were removed to the little churchyard at St. Paul's in Pendleton. Other Bee and Stevens family members were already there in a low-walled plot, and in a few years Peter Fayssoux made the trip to Mississippi and brought back the remains of his brother Navy Lieutenant Henry Kennedy Stevens.

THE CURTAIN HASN'T FALLEN YET

Peter Fayssoux was quite active in church work. Ellison Capers, who had withstood Sherman's siege on Atlanta, was in Charleston recovering from earlier injuries and Hamilton Bee still was in uniform in Texas. The Reverend Fayssoux Stevens was being introduced to the Reformed Episcopal Church, which was active in the North and in Canada. The Protestant Episcopal Church was not fully pursuing the black population in South Carolina. Bishop George David Cummins, a former Protestant Episcopalian, started the new order in 1874, and the only major difference in the two was that the new order welcomed all persons, including blacks.

Black communicants in South Carolina asked for entry into the Reformed order and before an answer could be received, they named Fayssoux to become "Pastor of All Colored Churches" in the state. Reverend Fayssoux Stevens was finding friends turning against him, but he moved forward.

In 1870 Hamilton Bee, who had moved back to Mexico after a post-military stay in Cuba, decided to go back to Texas. He said he and his family had stayed in Mexico partly by choice and partly from necessity. He wrote a friend that he seldom had enough to eat and he had sold his carriage, his horses, his furniture and his wife's silk dresses. He had lost the use of one eye and wrote he was "without means."

In 1876 changes were taking place in South Carolina. General Wade Hampton of Confederate note had been elected governor on the Democrat ticket, ridding the state of the Republican carpetbaggers and the moving out of Federal troops after a compromise with the national government. Ellison Capers became his secretary of education and he had double duty as he had become an Episcopal minister and was at Christ Church in Greenville.

The Reformed Episcopal Church needed a bishop in South Carolina, as one was necessary to perform the rite of Confirmation. Bishop Cummins had died in 1876. The result, in 1879, was the election of Peter Fayssoux Stevens as Missionary Bishop to the Special Jurisdiction of the South. Since blacks could not attend the white seminaries, Stevens began the Bishop Cummins Training School to prepare blacks for the priesthood. For many years, the school was in a suitcase and went wherever Fayssoux might be. He had also taken on the responsibility of becoming school commissioner for Charleston County and one of his acts was to announce an institute for black teachers. It was classed as the first such institute in the South.

In 1882, Ellison Capers was still rector at Christ Church in Greenville. That same year Hamilton Bee had gone to work at the new Agricultural and Mechanical College in Bryan, Texas. In South Carolina in 1889, an earthquake all but destroyed Charleston, something the Union soldiers could not do. Bishop Stevens said there was no loss of life among his members and little damage to the black churches. Education in South Carolina had been promised, but the government largely overlooked the black population when schools began cropping up. Seeing a need, Bishop Stevens led the founding of the Reformed Episcopal Parochial School, located on Nassau Street in Charleston.

Blacks had not totally been denied an education, however. While still under Republican military rule the legislature in 1872 created the College of Agriculture and Mechanics' Institute for Colored Students in Orangeburg, adjoining the female seminary there. That property was purchased by the Lee Claflin family of Boston and by 1890 the two schools were operating as one, under the Claflin name. Bishop Stevens was sixty years old in 1890, and he joined the Claflin faculty as professor of mathematics, continuing his church duties and bringing along the theological school in his suitcase.

One of Fayssoux's saddest times was in October 1891. Beside him during his struggles with his religious and educational work, the horrors of war and its aftermath was his wife of thirty-six years, Mary Singleton Capers Stevens, who died at age fifty-eight. Mary was the daughter of a Methodist bishop, the sister of a Protestant Episcopal minister who would become a bishop and the wife of a Reformed Episcopal bishop. The mother of nine children, four survived her and only three lived to maturity. Stevens remained at Claflin through the 1890 school year, and after Mary's death he wed Harriett Rebecca Palmer, daughter of Dr. John Palmer, a signer of the declaration of Secession. She proved to be a much-needed companion.

Ellison Capers, who had married Harriett's cousin Charlotte Rebecca Palmer, left Christ Church after twenty years and went to Selma, Alabama, for one year, then spent four years in Columbia. In 1893 he was elected bishop of the Protestant Episcopal Church of South Carolina.

Hamilton Prioleau Bee died on October 2, 1897, at his home in San Antonio, Texas, where he had retired. He was seventy-five years old, twice married and the father of twelve children. Both he and his second wife, Mary Mildred Tarver, are buried in the Confederate cemetery there.

There was a special day in 1903 for Fayssoux. With the death of a Citadel alumnus in California he had become the oldest living graduate. He was seventy-three years old and in failing health. He had even become blind, having to read by Braille or listening to his wife read to him for hours at a time. On January 9, 1910, the mantle of "oldest living graduate" at The Citadel would be passed to another man. The flag flew at half-staff that day and newspapers throughout the state headlined the death of Peter Fayssoux Stevens. Unlike his brothers in Pendleton, he is buried at Magnolia Cemetery in Charleston.

Clement Hoffman Stevens was the astute businessman and self-taught military leader. Henry Kennedy Stevens was the dashing sailor who traveled the world. Peter Fayssoux, when he first began teaching at The Citadel, had astronomy listed as one of his courses. Perhaps it was then he started looking to the heavens and found the guidance that led him to lead and care for so many on earth.

...And In Conclusion

Whew! That's been a lot of storytelling. I think it would have taken less time and effort to do it verbally, as I did all those years. This section is highly important, however, as it's where I thank all the people who should be recognized.

Hurley E. Badders. *Photo by Richard Smith.*

Remember the lady at the start of this writing who almost scared me to death when I made my first talk, and how much I liked her? She was Mrs. Lillie Ballard Westmoreland, who chaired the commission and who hired me. I owe her more gratitude than can ever be expressed for giving me the opportunity to pursue as a career what had been a hobby—history.

Then there's my best friend, whom I rarely see. James Brannock has been in Columbia for many years.

Our friendship began when he was with the South Carolina Chamber of Commerce doing tourism and I was in my early years in Pendleton. Almost weekly joke exchanges over the telephone ended when he pursued another career (with no toll-free telephone). When he went out on his own as an appraiser, e-mail had been invented and we were back in business! James has been an anchor for me during dark moments, and is always cheering me on. Thanks James, and by the way, have you heard the one about…

Book writing is not a singular activity. It takes many people to get the job done and among those who deserve thanks are book editor Jenny Kaemmerlen, who has been patient, understanding, a guidance counselor and who should get a raise in pay for putting up with me; and copyeditor Deb Carver, who has done a wonderful job in editing my text and has been a great help to me. To all others at The History Press involved with this book, I tip my hat. Longtime friend Richard Smith, an exceptional photographer and graphics technician and his computer whiz son Garrett get special thanks, too. (It's the young ones who know computers, isn't it.)

Appreciation also goes to special friend Kathi Gray and to Phyllis and Earl, Glenda and Randall. I can't forget the family, either. Daughter April has been a grand support person; her husband William McBride is mentioned because he had an ancestor who was in the Twenty-fourth Regiment. Son Lanier, his wife Joy and my grandson A.J. Badders (a future Major League baseball player) are thanked and would be thanked even more if they would move back from the Midlands. Barbara, my wife of more than fifty years, gets super thanks just for being there.

Finally, a great big thank you to all the people over the years who listened to my talks and encouraged me.

Please visit us at
www.historypress.net